CONCISE GLOSSARY OF GEOLOGY

AF201589

S.M. MATHUR

SCIENTIFIC® PUBLISHERS
New Delhi • Jodhpur

Published by :
Pawan Kumar Sharma
Scientific Publishers (India)
5-A, New Pali Road. P.O. Box 91
E-mail : info@scientificpub.com
www.scientificpub.co

Print 2026

S.M. Mathur
Formerly, Director, Geological Survey of India
B-15, Alokpuri, Ravindrapalli
LUCKNOW - 226 016 (U.P.) India

© Mathur, S.M., 2007

ISBN: 978-81-72334-61-1
eISBN: 978-93-87307-48-3

Lasertype set: Rajesh Ojha
Printed in India

TO THE REVERED MEMORY OF

PROFESSOR D.K. CHAKRAVARTI

WHO WAS A WALKING

CYCLOPAEDIA OF GEOLOGY

"Every other author may aspire to praise; the lexicographer can only hope to escape reproach.

— Samuel Johnson (1709-84)

PREFACE

There has been a great upsurge in the teaching and practice of Geology in India during the last few decades mainly because of development of mineral and petroleum industries. Soon after Independence, there were few universities teaching this subject, but thereafter, there has been an upsurge and now there are geology departments in most universities, and their numbers are growing. There is, however, a great dearth of Indian text and reference books. This work is designed as a much-needed aid to students, teachers and professionals alike.

Like any modern science, the science of Geology has its own nomenclature and terminology. Since it is an interdisciplinary science it has taken to its bosom terms also derived from physical, chemical and biological sciences—relevant words from these also find a place, as also words from peripheral disciplines. The aim of this work is to cover all essential terms used in different branches of the science and to provide concise but adequate definitions and information for each. Descriptions of only basic mineral groups and species are given, for there are more than 3700 minerals known. Similarly, the number of rock types runs into hundreds, and only the main groups are defined. Also avoided are stage names and names of Indian and other stratigraphic units which would have made the volume unwieldy. The basic stratigraphic units, system/period and above, and their nomenclature, classification and ages, are however listed, and follow the latest *International Stratigraphic*

Chart 2004 of the International Commission on Stratigraphy of the International Union of Geological Sciences. The International stratigraphic column is given as an Annexure. The evolving concepts of stratigraphic classification and nomenclature are reflected in the relevant definitions. In addition, some stratigraphic unit names found in geological literature or proposed elsewhere have also been included.

My grateful thanks are due to Messrs Aditya Agarwal and Ashutosh Agrawala for their assistance in procuring literature, to my daughter Archana for help with the computer, and to Mr. Vikram Rai for helping me with meticulous proof correction.

S.M. MATHUR

B-15 ALOKPURI
Ravindrapalli
Lucknow

NOTES ON USAGE

- Cross-references are indicated by an asterisk (*). Cross-references are not given to certain frequently occurring terms, like various rock or mineral types (igneous, quartz, etc.) and stratigraphical hierarchical terms (system, epoch, etc.).
- Synonym and terms for comparison are in **bold** face.
- Alternative spelling of terms are in round brackets **( )**.
- Alternative terms in an entry are separated by a slash (/).
- Various types of features or structures are described after the main heading, like different types of metamorphism and folds are itemised after the main heading of **Metamorphism** or **Fold**.
- Words having once-ligatured dipthongs, such as 'ae' are given in both the British and American usage, but some terms use only the American form where 'a' is omitted.
- The qualifier 'about' before numerical dates indicate that there is a very small factor of error (±) in the value given which is not mentioned. But in the Annexure the full numerical values as mentioned in the original ICS – 2004 are given.

ABBREVIATIONS

Cf.	=	Compare with (L. *confer*)
GTS	=	*A Geologic Time scale 1989* (Cambridge University Press)
ICS	=	International Commission on Stratigraphy of IUGS
IUGS	=	International Union of Geological Sciences
Ma	=	Million years (*maga-annum*, 10^6 years)
Pl.	=	Plural
Sing.	=	Singular
Sp. gr.	=	Specific gravity
Syn.	=	Synonym

CONCISE GLOSSARY OF GEOLOGY

A

Aa — *See* **Lava.**

Ablation — (1) The erosion of rock by wind action. (2) The process of removal, mainly of solid material, especially ice, by melting or evaporation.

Abrasion — The effect on a rock surface caused by mechanical impact and friction of solid rock fragments moved by running water, wind, ice, etc., that cause destruction of the rock surface.

Abrasive — A substance capable of polishing or grinding and cutting, which is often a mineral material such as *diatomite, *silica and *pumice.

Absolute age — The absolute age of a geological event, fossil or rock expressed in a unit of time, usually years. Often used as a *Syn.* of *isotopic age or *radiometric age, but may also be used to refer to ages obtained by other methods, such as counting of *varves, tree rings, etc.

Abyssal — Relating to or denoting the depths of the ocean below the 3500 m level. *Cf.* **Bathyal.**

Abyssal deposits — The solid matter which covers the floor of the *abyssal region of the ocean.

Abyssal plain — A very flat area of the deep ocean floor which may extend for more than 1000 km; it has typically slopes less than 1:1000, and is found off continental margins where sediments can enter the deep sea.

Accessory mineral — A mineral whose presence in a rock is not essential to its proper classification or nomenclature. *Cf.* **Essential mineral.**

Accidental inclusion — *Syn.* **Xenolith**.

Accretion — The process by which land grows in size or form by accumulation of sediments over a period of time.

Achrondite — *See* **Meteorite.**

Acid / Acidic rocks — Igneous rocks that contain 10 per cent or more free quartz (more than 60 per cent silica) and are composed predominantly of light-coloured minerals.

Acritarch — A unicellular, resistant-walled unicellular organic body of unknown or uncertain biological relationship and characterized by varied sculpture, some being smooth and others spiny; many of the acritarchs are of algal affinity but the group is artificial. They range from the *Precambrian to the *Holocene but are specially abundant in the Precambrian and the early *Palaeozoic.

Actinolite-Tremolite — Minerals of the *Amphibole group containing calcium, magnesium and iron, occurring chiefly in metamorphic rocks; monoclinic; prismatic, fibrous; green (actionlite), white (tremolite); fibrous varieties may become *asbestos.

Adit — A nearly horizontal passage from the surface of a mine.

Aeolian deposits — Deposits relating to or caused by wind. *See* also **Loess.**

Aeon — The alternative spelling of **Eon** — generally not in use.

Aerobic — Relating to organisms that require free oxygen to live.

Aerolite — *Syn.* of **Stony meteorite.**

Agate— A colour-banded variety of *chalcedony, or *cryptocrystalline form of silica.

Age — (1) The formal geochronologic unit of the lowest rank, below epoch. (2) A term used informally to designate a length of geologic time during which the rocks of any stratigraphic unit were formed. (3) An informal term for time during which any geological event took place marked by special physical conditions.

Agglomerate — Coarse volcanic rock consisting of a mixture of fragments of various sizes and shapes

Aggradation — The process which tends to build land surface by deposition of solid material by a stream or current

Aggregate — A mixture of sand, gravel, or slag used for mixing with cementing material to form concrete, mortar or plaster.

Alabaster — A fine-grained, translucent banded variety of *gypsum.

Albite — *See* **Plagioclase feldspars.**

Algae (Sing. **Alga**) — A group of primitive non-flowering and largely aquatic plants lacking roots, leaves and vascular tissues. The group includes *diatoms. Algae may secrete calcium carbonate to form *reefs. Algae range from the *Precambrian to the present day.

Alkali / Alkaline — Referring to igneous rocks and minerals that have high contents of the alkali metal oxides, Na_2O and K_2O. In alkali rocks sodic and / or *potassic **feldpars** are dominant. The term is also applied to rocks which contain essential *feldspathoids.

Alkali feldspars — A series of minerals with composition varying between the two end members *orthoclase ($KAlSi_3O_8$) and *albite ($NaAlSi_3O_8$); they include *microcline ($KAlSi_3O_8$), sanidine, and adularia. *See* **Feldspars.**

Allochems — Several varieties of discrete and organized carbonate aggregates forming coarser framework of grains comprising *fossils, *interclasts, *oolites, *pellets *pisolites and *sphelurites.

Allochthonous — Said of a deposit or formation that originated at a distance from its present position.

Allogenesis — The process by which a mineral or rock fragment derived from existing rock was formed at some distance from its present location.

Allotriomorphic — Said of a texture formed essentially by *anhedral grains. *Syn.* **Xenomorphic.**

Alloy — A metallic substance composed of two or more *metal *elements made by being fused together when molten.

Alluvium — Any unconsolidated, sorted or semisorted detritial material (clay, silt, sand, gravel, etc.) deposited during comparatively recent times by streams in their beds, flood plains, or deltas.

Alteration — (1) Any change in the mineralogical composition in a rock brought about by physical or chemical action, especially by the action of *hydrothermal solutions. (2) Changes in mineralogical or chemical composition in a rock or mineral as a result of weathering. (3) *Supergene changes in a rock or mineral.

Alumina — A major constituent of many clays, composition Al_2O_3; occurs native as mineral *corundum, and gem stones ruby (red) and sapphire (blue).

Amber — Fossil resin, translucent or transparent, frequently enclosing insects.

Amethyst — A clear purple or bluish violet variety of crystallized quartz used as a *semi-precious stone.

Ammonoidea/Ammonites — An extinct invertebrate mollusk, a subclass of *Cephalopoda, that was characterized by flat, thick, strongly ornamental spiral shell with sutures having finely divided lobes and saddles. Ammonites ranged from the Lower *Devonian, possibly Upper *Silurian, to Upper *Cretaceous, and have been used extensively as zonal indices in the *Mesozoic.

Amorphous — A substance which is apparently not crystalline.

Amphibia/Amphibians — A class of cold-blooded vertebrate animals intermediate in many characters between fishes and reptiles and characterized by gill-breathing aquatic larvae and terrestrial air-breathing adults. They include frogs, toads, newts, salamanders, and caecllians. They evolved in the Upper *Devonian times and occur even today.

Amphiboles — A group of hydrous rock-forming silicate mineral of considerable chemical complexity, characterized structurally by a double-chain of linked SiO_4 tetrahedra, with iron, magnesium, calcium, sodium and aluminium among the elements which may be present between the chains. Common varieties include *hornblende, *actinolite and *tremolite; fibrous forms belong to the *asbestos group of minerals.

Amphibolite — A crystallized metamorphic rock composed mainly of *amphibole and *plagioclase with little or no *quartz, resulting from regional metamorphism of basic igneous rocks or of impure calcareous sediments.

Amphineura — A small class of marine *Mollusca which have reduced head, mantle cavity all round foot and head, eight shell plates over visceral hump. They are found from the Late *Cambrian to the present day.

Amygdale / Amygdule — A spheroidal or elliptical *vesicle in an igneous rock containing secondary minerals often in a zonal arrangement.

Amygdaloidal — Said of a volcanic rock in which the openings are filled with secondary minerals.

Anaerobic — Biological forms that live, are active, and occur or exist in the absence of free oxygen.

Analcite / Analcime — A whitish feldspathoid, composition $NaAl.Si_2O_6(H_2O)$; cubic; hardness 5; sp. gr. 2.3.

Analysis — A process, often chemical, for separation of a whole into its component parts.

Analyzer — It is the polarizing mechanism such as the upper *Nicol prism or *Polaroid that is a part of a *petrological microscope where the light is intersected after it has passed through the slide under study. *Cf.* **Polarizer.**

Anatase — A mineral of titanium, TiO_2; tetragonal; tabular; hardness 5.5; sp. gr. 3.9.

Anatexis — In petrology, *in situ* partial melting of pre-existing rocks. *Syn.* **Palingenesis.**

Andalusite — A white mineral of aluminium silicate (Al_2SiO_5); orthorhombic; hardness 7.5; sp. gr. 3.2; found in metamorphic rocks. It is used as an indicator of the pressure and temperature of *metamorphism in rocks. It is trimorphous with **Kyanite** and **Sillimanite.**

Andesine — *See* **Plagioclase feldspars**

Andesite — A fine-grained, intermediate, *volcanic rock of intermediate composition containing *plagioclase feldspar with *biotite, *hornblende or *pyroxene chemically equivalent to *diorite. When porphyritic, *phenocrysts are generally composed of the same minerals as those of the *groundmass.

Angaraland — A name for a small shield exposing *Precambrian rocks in north-central Siberia that existed in the *Caboniferous and *Permian times and that was supposed to have been the vertex or high point around which all other structures of Asia were built.

Angiosperm — A plant of a large group that comprises those that have flowers and produce seeds enclosed within a carpel; it includes herbaceous plants, shrubs, grasses and most trees. Such plants first appeared in Early *Cretaceous or possibly earlier and continue to the present.

Angular unconformity — The unconformity is characteristic of sedimentary rocks that are laid upon previously tilted or folded strata; bedding planes below and above the unconformity surface are at an angle to each other.

Anhedral — Said of a crystal having no plane faces. *Syn.* **Xenomorphic; Allotriomorphic.**

Anhydrite — A white evaporite mineral consisting of anhydrous calcium sulphate ($CaSO_4$); orthorhombic; fibrous/granular; hardness 3.5; sp. gr. 2.9.

Anisotropic — Having different physical properties when measured in different directions. Crystals belonging to systems other than the cubic are optically anisotropic and exhibit double *refraction, or *birefringence.

Ankerite — A dolomitic iron-containing carbonate mineral, $CaFe(CO_3)_2$; trigonal; hardness of 3.5–4; sp. gr. 2.95–3.1.

Annelida/Annelids — A large phylum of invertebrate animals like worms that is comprised of a segmented body and distinct head. Because of their largely soft parts they are known only from their burrows and trails, and are of little geological importance.

Anorthite — *See* **Plagioclase feldspars.**

Anorthosite — A coarse-grained *plutonic igneous rock composed essentially of *plagioclase feldspar with minor *ferromagnesian minerals.

Antecedent stream — A stream that was established before the local uplift and in spite of the uplift maintained its original course all the time by incising its channel at about the same rate as the land was rising.

Anthozoa — A class of *Coelenterata whose body is a *polyp and there is no medusa stage; they may have an external calcareous skeleton forming *coral. They range from the *Precambrian to the present.

Anthracite — *Coal of the highest rank; it is a hard lustrous variety containing more than 90% carbon, and little volatile matter.

Anticline — A flexure in stratified rocks which is convex or arched upward with its limbs dipping outwards from the crest and in which the oldest strata form the core and the younger beds get younger towards the top. It is opposite of **Syncline.**

Anticlinorium — A composite anticlinal structure on regional scale consisting of a set of smaller folds.

Antiform — A flexture in stratified rocks which is convex or arched upward with its limbs dipping outwards from its crest but the stratigraphic sequence of its beds is not known. The opposite is **Synform.**

Apatite — A phosphate mineral of composition $Ca_5(F,Cl)(PO_4)_3$; hexagonal; prism/pyramid; granular; hardness 5; sp. gr. 3.2; mostly green in colour.

Aphanetic — Said of a texture of a very fine-grained volcanic igneous rock made up of crystals too small to be resolved by the naked eye. It includes **Microcrystalline** and **Cryptocrystalline** textures.

Aplite — A light-coloured, fine-grained igneous rock of mainly granitic composition with minerals quartz, feldspars and *muscovite.

Aquamarine — A gem variety of **Beryl**, refractive index 1.568–1.602/ 1.568–1.6025; birefringence 0.005–0.009; dispersion 0.014.

Aquifer —Water-bearing strata with high porosity and permeability.

Aquifer, Artesian — Same as **Aquifer, Confined.**

Aquifer, Confined — An aquifer bounded above and below by impervious layers that restrict it. *Syn.* **Artesian aquifer**. Also *See* **Artesian well.**

Aragonite — White to grayish carbonate mineral, composition $CaCO_3$; orthorhombic; pseudo-hexagonal; hardness 3.5–4; sp. gr. 2.94. It is trimorphous with *calcite and *vaterite (a rare, unstable carbonate mineral)

Archaean (Archean) — Older of the two eons/eonothems in which the *Precambrian was divided earlier. Considered the period of time from the formation of the Earth believed at about 4560 million of years ago to the start of the *Proterozoic 2500 Ma ago, it is now considered by ICS-2004 to overlie the *Hadean, but its lower limit is not defined though it is taken at about 3850 Ma ago on the basis of the oldest preserved *supracrustals. Its fourfold subdivisions are *Eoarchean (lower limit not defined), Paleoarchean (base 3600 Ma), Mesoarchean (base 3200 Ma), and Neoarchean (base 2800 Ma, upper limit 2500 Ma, lying under *Siderian of the *Proterozoic).

Archaeocyatha — A phylum of invertebrate animals characterized by a calcareous inverted cone-shaped skeleton. They are completely extinct and are found in rocks of the Lower *Cambrian to the Middle *Ordovician.

Archaeozoic (Archeozoic) — An **obsolete** term for an era of the *Precambrian, following the **Eozoic** and preceding the *Ptoterozoic.

Arenaceous — Said of a sedimentary rock, loose or consolidated, which contains sand or sand-like particles.

Arenites— Sandy sedimentary rock group that includes *sandstones, *greywackeys, *arkoses, *greensands (glauconitic/chloritic) and *calcarenites. *Syn.* **Psammites.**

Argillite — A compact mudstone (claystone or siltstone) or *shale that has undergone a somewhat higher degree of *induration, composed entirely of *clay minerals,

Argentiferous — Rocks or minerals containing silver.

Argentite — A valuable ore of silver, composition Ag_2S; cubic; octahedral; hardness 2–2.5; sp. gr. 7.20–7.36; metallic lustre. Also known as 'silver glance'.

Argillaceous — Said of a sedimentary rock containing a substantial portion of *clay minerals.

Arkose — A coarse-grained *sandstone which has at least 25 per cent *feldspar.

Arsenopyrite — A sulphide mineral of arsenic, composition FeAsS; orthorhombic; prismatic; hardness 5.5-6; sp. gr. 6; also massive and granular.

Artesian well — A well in which water is under pressure and the water flows to the surface naturally.

Arthropoda / Arthropods — A large phylum of invertebrate animals having a segmented body, external skeleton, and joined limbs, including insects, spiders, and crustaceans. Of the large number of groups, *Trilobita, *Eurypteida, *Ostrocoda, and *Crustacea are geologically important.

Asbestos — Any of highly heat-resistant silicate minerals (like *amphiboles tremolite or actinolite, or serpentine chrysolite) that separates into long flexible fibers.

Ash, volcanic — *Tephra fragments less than 2 mm in size ejected during a volcanic eruption.

Ashlar — A block of building stone cut and dressed with straight edges.

Assay — Analysis of ore to determine the presence and quantity of one or more specific component.

Asthenosphere — The soft, heated upper rock layer of the *Mantle immediately below the rigid *Lithosphere, in which there is relatively low resistance to plastic flow which allows the lithospheric *plates to move slowly about the Earth's surface.

Atoll — A roughly circular structure of coral reefs enclosing a lagoon.

Attrition — The process of mutual wear and tear caused by running water, wind, ice, waves, etc., that loosen rock particles and fragments and then decreases their size and increases their roundness through continual rubbing, grinding, knocking, scraping, and bumping against each other.

Augen — A large, eye-shaped crystal, commonly of feldspar, which develops in quartzo-feldspathic bands of some *gneisses.

Augite — An aluminous, usually black or dark green pyroxene, composition $(Ca,Mg,Fe,Al)_2$ $(Al,Si)_2O_6$; monoclinic; prismatic; hardness 6; sp. gr. 3.4 .

Auguclast — An angular *phenoclast, such as a fragment in a *breccia.

Aulacogen — A narrow, sediment-filled basin that extends into a *craton either from a *geosyncline or from a mountain belt that formed from a geosyncline.

Authigenesis — The process by which a constituent mineral of a rock that is formed *in situ* during or after the formation of the rock in which it lies.

Autochthonous — Said of a deposit or formation formed in its present position.

Autoclast — A fragment in an *autoclastic rock which is broken or brecciated *in situ* as a result of some mechanical process.

Autoclastic — Term for fragments formed by mechanical friction during movement of lava, or gravity crumbling of spires or domes.

Autogeosyncline — A *parageosyncline without a marginal uplifted area containing mostly carbonate sediments.

Autolith — An inclusion in an igneous rock that was formed at the same time or to which it is genetically related. *Syn.* **Cognate inclusion.**

Automorphic — Same as **Euhedral.**

Aves (Birds) — The class of vertebrates which comprise the birds that evolved from the reptiles but lost many of their reptilian characters. They first appeared in the Upper *Jurassic and continue to the present.

Axial plane — (1) A plane that passes the successive *hinge lines of the beds in a *fold. (2)A plane that contains two crystallographic axes.

Axis — (1) In structural geology, the line which approximates the shape of any *fold when moved parallel to itself. (2) In paleontology, the median lobe of a trilobite. (3) In crystallography, one of the three imaginary lines in a crystal (four in a hexagonal crystal) that passes through its center and is used as a reference to describe a crystal structure and symmetry.

Azoic — A disused term for the entire *Precambrian, or for the *Archaean. (The earlier part of the Precambrian where the rocks did not contain traces of life.) *Cf.* **Archaeozoic; Cryptozoic.**

Azurite — A deep blue carbonate mineral of copper, $2CuCO_3.Cu(OH)_2$; monoclinic; massive; hardness 4; sp. gr. 3.77–3.83.

B

Badlands — A region marked by extensive incision and heavy erosion of unconsolidated sediments forming deep gullies and ravines, separated by steep ridges.

Ball and pillow — Oblate spheroids or ellipsoids, or kidney-shaped *sandstone or *limestone bodies surrounded by finer sand or silt.

Ballast — Crushed rock used on railway tracks or for forming road beds. *Cf.* **Road metal.**

Banded iron formation (BIF) — An iron-rich sedimentary rock composed of layers of hematite and cherty beds. Same as Banded hematite-quartzite (BHQ).

Barchan (Barkhan, Barchane) — A crescent-shaped *Sand Dune, with horns of the crescent projecting down-wind.

Barytes (Barite) — A colourless mineral, composition, $BaSO_4$; orthorhombic; hardness 3; sp. gr. 4.5.

Basalt — A dark-coloured, fine-grained basic volcanic igneous rock, low in silica, made up chiefly of calcic *plagioclase and *clinopyroxene and in many cases, of *olivine.

Base metals — In mining industry the term for metals copper, lead and zinc.

Base map — A topographic map, already printed or specially prepared, on which geological information is plotted.

Basement — The oldest formation of rocks underlying a particular area of stratified rocks.

Basic rocks — Dark-coloured igneous rocks that are quartz-free and generally contain more calcic than sodic *feldspars (silica 44 – 51%), commonly contain pyroxenes and olivine, and small quantities of *hornblende and *biotite; they are mainly composed of dark-coloured minerals.

Basin — A large depression, erosional or structural, in which sedimentation often takes place.

Batholith — A very large mass of igneous rock, typically *granite, intruded while molten into the surrounding *country rock, outcropping over a large area and extending to unknown depth.

Bathyal — Referring to continental slope between 200 and 3500 m depths of the ocean. *Cf.* **Abyssal**

Bauxite — An amorphous clayey rock that is the chief ore of aluminium, and consists of hydrated aluminium with variable proportion of iron oxides.

Bearing — The direction or position of a feature relative to a fixed point, normally measured in degrees with a *compass showing the magnetic north as zero (0°).

Becke line — A line on a margin of grain in thin section immersed in a liquid seen under the petrological microscope which moves into the medium of higher index of refraction and is thus used to determine relative index of refraction between grains.

Bed — (1) The smallest formal unit in the hierarchy of sedimentary *lithostraigraphic unit, e.g., a single *stratum lithologically distinct from other layers above and below, and given a distinguishing name. (2) A tabular or lenticular form of a sedimentary rock that is greater than one cm in thickness. It is also called a *stratum. A layer less than one cm is called a *lamina. Classification of beds along with splitting terms is as follows —

< 2	mm	Fissile	Very thinly laminated
2–10	mm	Fissile	Thinly laminated
1–3	cm	Flaggy	Very thinly bedded
3–10	cm	Flaggy	Thinly bedded
10–30	cm	Slabby	Medium bedded
30–100	cm	Blocky	Thickly bedded
>100	cm	Massive	Very thickly bedded

Bedding — The fundamental feature of layering or stratification of a sedimentary rock.

Bedrock — A general term for usually unweathered solid rock lying beneath unconsolidated superficial material. Not to be confused with **Country rock**.

Belemnoidea/Belemnites — Extinct mollusk invertebrates, a subgroup of *Cephalopoda group, that had bullet-shaped well-developed internal shell. They ranged from the *Mississippian to the *Eocene and were important fossils from rocks of the *Mesozoic when their best development took place.

Beneficiation — The process of treatment of ore to separate the desired mineral from the gangue in preparation for smelting.

Benioff zone — The inclined seismic zone within the Earth's *lithosphere extending down at an angle of 45° from the base of an oceanic trench to the *asthenosphere, dipping toward and beneath volcanic arcs. It is typical of destructive *plate margins where one plate overrides another as a result of *sea-floor spreading and consumes ocean floors.

Benthic (Benthonic) — Relating to the marine life zone at the bottom of the sea floor, distinguished from **Pelagic.**

Bentonite — An absorptive and colloidal clay mainly consisting of *montmorillonite formed by the alteration of tuff or volcanic ash.

Beryl — A beryllium, aluminium silicate mineral, composition $Be_3Al_2Si_6O_{18}$; hexagonal prism; hardness 7.5-8; sp. gr. 2.63-2.8 (varying). It occurs in granitic *pegmatites sometimes of enormous size. Transparent gem varieties are the green *emerald; and the blue *aquamarine.

Bhit — Indian term for a longitudinal sand ridge or hill. *Cf.* **Seif.**

Biaxial — Said of a crystal having two optic axes and three principal indices of refraction, in minerals belonging to orthorhombic, monoclinic or triclinic crystal systems. The phenomenon is observed under a polarizing microscope.

Binomial nomenclature. The method of naming species of animals and plants —both living and fossil — scientifically, consisting of the name of the *genus flowed by the name of the *species. The full name is printed in italics; the genus name is capitalized, and the species name is in lower case.

Bioclast — A fragment of skeletal material or organisms in limestone.

Biocoenosis — An assemblage of fossil remains found in the same place where the organisms lived and died.

Biofacies — A distinct assemblage of fossil organisms formed under one set of environmental conditions in a subdivision of a stratigraphic unit.

Bioherm — A mass or *reef of organic material built by calcareous remains of sedentary organisms, such as algae, corals, crinoids, foraminifers, mollusks, stromatoporoids, etc.

Biolith — A rock of organic origin or composed of organic remains, such as *Coal or *Bitumen.

Biostratigraphy — The branch of *stratigraphy that deals with the distribution of fossils in the stratigraphic record and the organization of strata into units on the basis of their contained fossils.

Biostrome — An extensive, clearly-bedded or sheet-like mass of rock built by and derived from the remains of sedentary organisms, such as a bed of *corals, *crinoids, *shells, etc.

Biota — Collective term for animal and plant population of a region, habitat or geological period.

Biotite — A generally black *mica, silicate of iron, magnesium, potassium and aluminium; monoclinic; prismatic; hardness 2.5–3; sp. gr. 2.7–3.1.

Bioturbation — In trace fossils the reworking or disruption of biogenic or physical stratification of sediments by the activity of an organism.

Biozone — A general term for any kind of biostratigraphic unit regardless of thickness or geographical extent, or time span.

Birefringence — The property of crystals other than those of the *cubic system to split a beam of ordinary light into two beams of unequal velocities, the difference between the greatest and the least indicies of refraction of a crystal. *Syn.* **Double refraction.**

Bitumen — A general term for natural inflammable substance principally of a mixture of *hydrocarbons.

Bivalvia — *See* **Lamellibranchiata.**

Black cotton soil — *See* **Regur**.

Blastomylonitic — A texture of recrystallised, tectonically sheared *mylonitic rock which has grown new crystals of larger size during *metamorphism.

Block lava — *See* **Lava**.

Blue ground — *Syn.* of **Kimberlite.**

Blueshist facies — A low temperature, high-pressure metamorphic facies in which the *amphibole glaucophane is typically present.

Bluff — A kind of cliff that has almost a perpendicular front overlooking a plain, sometimes hanging over the rock underneath

Boart (Bort) — Imperfectly crystallized or flawed diamond or diamond fragments used as abrasive.

Boghead coal — A *sapropelic coal resembling *cannel coal in its physical properties but consisting dominantly of algal matter rather than *spores.

Bole — A fine, compact, friable, earthy clay, usually coloured red, brown or yellow due to the presence of iron oxide, and consisting essentially of hydrous aluminium, or less often of magnesium; it is a decomposition product of basaltic rocks..

Bolson — An extensive alluvial basin or depression into which drainage from surrounding mountains flow centripetally with gentle gradient towards a playa or central depression.

Bomb, Volcanic — Rounded to subrounded large fragments of lava thrown out in a plastic or viscous condition during a volcanic eruption.

Boninite — In IUGS classification a volcanic rock (*pillow lava) consisting of *olivine and *pyroxene, poor in *plagioclase feldspar with accessory magnesiochromite in a glassy *groundmass.

Bornhardt — *Syn.* of **Inselberg.**

Botryoidal — Having a rounded bunch of grapes-like form.

Bottomset — *See* **Cross bedding.**

Boudin — A series of elongated parallel sections formed by the fracturing of a hard sedimentary rock *stratum during folding.

Bouguer anomaly — A gravity anomaly that takes into account the effect of topography but not isostatic compensation.

Boulder — (1) A detached, rounded and much-worn mass of rock. (2) As a size term all rock particles above 256 mm in diameter are included in it.

Boulder clay — *Syn.* of **Till.**

Bouma Cycle — A fixed, charecteristic succession of five intervals that makes up a complete sequence of a *turbiditie, though one or more of the intervals may be missing. The five intervals are, from bottom to top: (i) graded, (ii) lower parallel laminations, (iii) current ripple laminations, (iv) upper parallel laminations, and (v) peletic.

Brachiopoda / Brachiopods — A phylum of marine invertebrate animals with bivalve shells within which are a pair of arms bearing tentacles used to capture food to the mouth. The shells are generally unequal in size but symmetrical. They occur from the Lower *Cambrian to the present.

Brass — A yellow *alloy essentially of copper and zinc in variable proportions.

Breccia — Coarse sedimentary rock made up of a mixture of angular rocks cemented by a finer-grained *matrix.

Brittle — The property of a hard mineral which has a tendency to shatter easily on impact.

Bronze — A yellowish *alloy of copper with up to one-third tin, sometimes of other elements too.

Brown coal. *Syn.* of **Lignite**

Brunton compass — A special pocket *compass for the use of a geologist that consists of an ordinary compass together with a spirit level *clinometer for reading vertical and horizontal angles.

Bryophyta / Bryophyte — A division of nonvascular plants that may have differentiated stems and leaves but have no true roots. They range from Upper *Carboniferous to the present.

Bryozoa — A phylum of small, aquatic, mostly marine, invertebrate animals with calcareous skeleton that typically forms mossy colonies comprising a few million individuals. They are abundant as fossils, and range from *Ordovician (possibly Late *Cambrian) to the present. *Syn.* **Polyzoa.**

Butte — An isolated, flat-topped, steep-sided landmass standing distinctly above the surrounding country similar to a **Mesa** but much smaller, and often produced from a mesa when it gets reduced in size through *erosion and dissection.

Bytownite — *See* **Plagioclase feldspars.**

C

Calc-alkaline rocks — Such igneous rocks in which the dominant *feldspar is calcium-rich. Such rocks tend to contain calcium-bearing *ferromagnesian minerals like *hornblende, *augite, etc. *Cf.* **Alkali / Alkaline.**

Calcarenite — A *clastic limestone of average grain size (particles between 0.06 mm and 2.0 mm) between that of *calcilutite and *calcirudite

Calcareous rocks — Rocks, that are made of *carbonate minerals.

Calcification — (1) The process of hardening of soft organic tissue by deposition of or conversion into calcium carbonate or some other insoluble calcium compound during fossilization. (2) Deposition of calcium carbonate near the surface of the soil through capillary action, leaving behind an accumulation of solid calcium carboate. *See* also **Reh.**

Calcilutite — A *clastic limestone of average grain size less than that of *calciarenite (less than 0.06 mm)

Calcirudite — A *clastic limestone of average grain size larger than that of *calcarenite (greater than 2 mm).

Calcite — Carbonate mineral, composition $CaCO_3$; trigonal; prismatic; hardness 3; sp. gr. 2.71; generally white in colour. It is trimorphous with *aragonite and *vaterite.

Calcrete — Another term for **Caliche**. In India called **Kankar.**

Caldera — A large basin-shaped *crater bounded by steep cliffs, usually formed by the subsidence of the top of a volcanic mountain, sometimes occupied by a lake.

Caliche — Lime-rich deposits formed in soils of certain semi-arid regions. *Syn.* **Calcrete.**

Calymmian — The lower *geochronometric subdivision of the *Mesoproterozoic dated between 1600 and 1400 Ma ago, lying above the *Statherian and below the *Ectasian.

Cambrian — The earliest geological system / period of the *Paleozoic (start of the *Phanerozoic) lasting from about 542.0 to about

488.3 Ma ago. It consists of three series / epoch. It was characterized by widespread seas, much volcanic activity and long periods of sedimentation; its rocks contain a large variety of marine invertebrate fossils including *trilobites and *brachiopods.

Canada balsam — A yellowish resin obtained from the balsam fir, used for mounting specimens on microscope slides; it has a refractive index of 1.54.

Canga — A well-consolidated, unstratified, iron-rich surfacial deposit.

Canyon — A large, deep, narrow gorge or valley bounded by steep slopes, often with a stream flowing though it.

Cap rock — An impermeable layer of shale or other rock overlying and sealing an oil or gas reservoir.

Carapace — A bony or chitinous hard case or shield covering the back or part of the back of an animal.

Carbonaceous — Relating to, containing, or composed of carbon.

Carbonado — An impure opaque dark-coloured, fine-grained aggregate of diamond particles that is very tough..

Carbonates / Carbonate minerals — Minerals with CO_3 as fundamental unit in their structure. The group includes hydrous carbonates *malachite (green) and *azurite (blue).

Carbonatite — A carbonate rock of magmatic origin, often accompanied by *rare earth minerals. Their origin is controversial.

Carboniferous — The system/period of the *Paleozoic between the *Devonian and the *Permian, extending from about 359.2 Ma to about 299.0 Ma ago. It was characterized by sea beds rising to form new land areas with extensive swampy forests of conifers and ferns which now form most of the present day *coal deposits. It had abundant *amphibians and sharks as well as widespread *coral reefs and limestone deposits; also *reptiles and seed-bearing plants first appeared during this time. In North America it is divided into the *Mississippian and the *Pennsylvanian.

Carborandum — A very hard black solid consisting of silicon carbide used as an *abrasive.

Cassiterite — A brownish, reddish or black mineral, chief source of metallic tin, SnO_2; tetragonal; prismatic; hardness 6.5; sp. gr. 7.

Cataclasis — Deformation of rock accomplished by fracture and rotation of rigid mineral grains or aggregates without chemical reconstitution and in which the strength of the material increases.

Cataclastic — A structure produced by the action of severe mechanical stress resulting in bending, breaking and granulation of minerals due to dynamic metamorphism.

Cataclastic rocks — Rocks that have undergone mechanical breakage or deformation, such as **Fault breccias**, and **Mylonites.**

Cement — (1) Mineral material that occurs in the spaces among the individual grains of a consolidated sedimentary rock, thereby binding the grains together in as a cohesive and rigid mass. (2) A powdery material made by calcining lime and clay used in mortar and concrete; also called 'Portland cement'.

Cenozoic (Cainozoic) — The youngest of the three erathems/eras of the *Phanerozoic starting 65.5 Ma ago and extending to the present, now subdivided by ICS-2004 into two, viz., *Palaeogne and *Neogene. Earlier, ICS-2000 had classified it into three systems/periods of *Palaeogene, *Neogene and *Quaternary. Traditionally, before the exercises undertaken to standardize the Geologic Time Scale by ICS of IUGS, the Cenozoic was classified into two systems/periods known as the *Tertiary and the *Quaternary. Both these unit terms have now been discarded by ICS. The Cenozoic was characterized by widespread changes in fauna, with the evolution and dominance of mammals, advanced mollusks and birds and flowering plants, and the development of the present-day geographical features.

Centripetal — A structural basin in which the dips converge inwards towards a central depression. (2) A pattern of drainage in which the streams converge inwards a central depression like a *basin, *bolson or *crater.

Cephalopoda / Cephalopods — A class of marine *Mollusca with well-developed head with a crown of mobile tentacles; mantle cavity posterior. The class includes sub-class *Nautiloidea, *Ammonoidea, and *Belemnoidea..

Chalcedony — A *cryptocrystalline form of silica (SiO_2) such as *agate, *chert, *flint, or *jasper.

Chalcocite — A black or gray lustrous copper ore, Cu_2S; orthorhombic; massive; hardness 3; sp. gr. 5.7.

Chalcopyrite — A brass yellow, important copper ore, $CuFeS_2$; tetragonal; massive; hardness 3.5–4; sp. gr. 4.2.

Chalk — A soft, earthy, usually white carbonate rock, $CaCO_3$, composed chiefly of the skeletal remains of foraminifers.

Charnockite — A coarse, hypersthene-bearing granitic (quartz-feldspar) rock. In India it is considered a part of a whole series of rocks varying in composition from acidic to ultrabasic found in a particular region.

Chert — An amorphous or microscopically fine-grained form of silica (SiO_2), often colour-banded.

China clay — Commercial name of kaolin, a mineral of *kaolinite group.

Chlorite — A dark green aluminosilicate of magnesium and iron; monoclinic; scaly / platy; hardness 2.5; sp. gr. about 3.

Chondrite — *See* **Meteorite.**

Chordata/Chordates — A large phylum of animals that includes the *vertebrates together with the sea squirts and lancelets, distinguished by possessing a notochord (a cartilaginous skeletal rod supporting the body in all embryonic and some adult chordate animals). The animals have widely differing morphologies, ranging from sessile sea squirts to humans. Of the several groups of the Chordata, only two are of some geological importance, namely, **Graptolithina** and **Vertebrata.**

Chromite — An ore of chromium containing iron, $FeCr_2O_4$; cubic; massive; hardness 5.5–6; sp. gr. 4.6; brownish black in colour.

Chron — The interval of geological time during which the rocks of a *chronozone were formed.

Chronology — A discipline of science that deals with arrangement of events or dates in the order of their occurrence.

Chronostratigraphic unit — A body of rocks that include all rocks formed during a specific interval of geologic time, and only those rocks formed during that time span. The rank and relative magnitude of the units in the chronostratigraphic hierarchy are a function of the length of time interval that their rocks subtend, rather than their physical thickness. The hierarchy of ranked chronostratigraphic units along with equivalent **Geochronologic units** is given below:

Chronostratigraphic	*Geochronologic*
Eonothem	**Eon**
Erathem	**Era**
System	**Period**
Series	**Epoch**
Stage	**Age**
Substage	**Subage**

Chronostratigraphy — The element of *stratigraphy that deals with the relative time and ages of rock bodies.

Chronozone — A non-hierarchical, commonly small, *chronostratigraphic unit, whose boundaries may be independent of those of ranked units.

Cinder — A vitreous vesicular *pyroclastic fragment that has fallen to the ground in an essentially solid condition.

Cinnabar — A mercury mineral, HgS; hexagonal; tabular; hardness 2–2.5; sp. gr. 8.1; red to brown in colour.

CIPW normative classification — A system of classifying igneous rocks based upon chemical composition of an igneous or metamorphic rock expressed in terms of standard minerals, the proportions of which form a basis for comparison and classification. Named after Cross, Iddings, Pirsson and Washington, American geologists. *Norm is different from *Mode, which is the actual mineral composition of a rock.

Cirque — A bowel-shaped, steep-sided hollow formed at the head of a mountain valley by the erosion of ice in glaciated regions.

Cisuralian — The lowest series / epoch of the three-fold *Permian, extending from about 299.0 to about 270.6 Ma, lying above the *Carboniferous and below the *Guadalupian, It consists of four stages.

Clarain — A coal material which is semi-bright, has silky lustre, and sheet-like irregular fracture.

Clast — A constituent fragment or grain of a *clastic rock.

Clastic rock — A rock made up of *clasts that include most of sedimentary rocks.

Clay — (1) Minerlogically, it is a group of hydrous silicates, mainly of aluminium and magnesium, occurring as platy and fibrous crystals that have a layered structure and the ability to take up and lose water. Clay minerals are the main constituents of argillaceous rocks, and are divided into four groups: *Kaolinite, *Illite, *Montmorillonite, and *Vermiculite. (2) As a size term, it is a particle smaller than 1/256 mm.

Clay gall — A roughly rounded or flattened fragment of *clay embedded generally in a sandy bed.

Clay minerals — A group of minerals with complex chemical composition. They are subdivided into the following subgroups; (i) *Kaolinite, (ii) *Illite, (iii) *Montmorillonite, and (iv) *Vermiculite.

Cleavage — (1) The tendency of a rock to split into closely-spaced planar structures as a result of deformation or metamorphism; the direction of cleavage is occasionally parallel to the stratification of the rocks, but is usually inclined or at right angles to it. (2) The character of a mineral to split along more or less a smooth surface in a linear plane generally parallel to a crystal face; it is controlled by the internal structure of the crystal.

Cliff — A high, very steep, perpendicular or overhanging rock face, either along a coastline or inland, mainly formed by *erosion.

Clinker — (1) A coal that has been altered by igneous intrusion. (2) A pyroclastic or autobrecciated fragment, rough and jagged in form, that resembles the *slag of a furnace.

Clinometer — A devise to measure the dip or inclination of strata, joints, slopes, etc. It may be a pendulum-like devise free-moving against a graduated arc, or may be a spirit level so mounted that the inclination could be read against a circular scale.

Clint — (1) A slab of limestone, parallel to the bedding, forming a pavement. (2) A hard or flinty rock forming a cliff.

Coal — A stratified, readily combustible rock containing more than 50% by weight and more than 70% by volume of carbonaceous material, formed from compaction and induration during burial of various fossil plant remains. The individual constituents of coals are known as *macerals. The various grades of coalification are as follows:*Peat→*Lignite (brown coal)→*Sub-bituminous→*Bituminous→*Sub-anthracite→*Anthracite.

Coal, Bituminous — A dark brown to black *coal that contains more than 14% volatile matter, and burns with a smoky flame.

Coal, Cannel — A *sapropelic massive coal consisting dominantly of *spores and *pollens containing much volatile matter that burns brightly. *Cf.* **Boghead coal.**

Coal, Humic — Coal that is of heterogenic origin and is banded with organic layers of diverse origin.

Coal, Grade of — Coals classified according to the degree of purity, i.e., quantity of inorganic material or ash left after burning.

Coal, Rank of — Grouping of coals according to degree of metamorphism; it is the basis of coal classification into a natural series from *lignite to *anthracite.

Coal, Type of — Classification of coals according to constituent plant materials.

Coal gas — Fuel produced by gasification of certain types of coals.

Coal gas methane — *See* **Methane.**

Coal measures — The group of rocks in a coalfield comprising coal seams, intevening strata of clay, sandstone, etc.

Coal seam — A stratum or bed of coal of any dimension.

Cobaltite — A grayish to silver white cobalt sulphur arsenide, CoAsS, cubic; massive, granular; hardness 5.5; sp. gr. 6–6.3.

Cobble — (1) A small round stone. (2) As a size term it is a particle between *pebble and *boulder, 64–256 mm in diameter.

Cocoliths — Minutiae calcareous plates that formed a protective covering of a group of unicellular organisms variously assigned to the *Algae or *Protozoa. They appeared in Late *Cambrian, and were common in the *Mesozoic, especially the *Cretaceous.

Coelenterata / Coelenterate — A phylum of aquatic, mostly marine, multicelled invertebrate animals that include hydroids, jellyfish, sea anemones, corals, and comb-jellies. They can be divided into three main classes, the *Scyphozoa, the *Hydrozoa,and the *Anthozoa.

Cognate inclusion — *Syn.* of **Autolith**.

Coke — A type of solid fuel produced by driving off the coal's volatile matter by heating in the absence of air.

Coking coal — A coal suitable for production of *coke for metallurgical purpose.

Colluvium — A loose, incoherent or heterogeneous soil material and/or rock fragments transported by rain wash or gravity and deposited at the base of a gentle slope or hillside.

Columnar jointing — A series of hexagonal or pentagonal joints resulting in columns of massive igneous rocks, particularly *basalts.

Compass — An instrument containing a magnetized needle which shows the direction of *magnetic north and the bearing from it.

Complex — A lithostratigraphic unit composed of diverse types of any class or classes of rocks (sedimentary, igneous, metamorphic) and characterized by irregularly mixed lithology or by highly complicated structural relations. All the words of a complex are capitalized. Example: Banded-Gneissic Complex.

Compound — A distinct substance formed by the chemical union of two or more elements in definite or fixed proportions.

Conchoidal fracture — Smoothly curving, concave or convex, surface of certain minerals on fracturing.

Concrete — A hard and strong building material made by mixing Portland *cement with a mineral *aggregate.

Concretion — An object similar to a *nodule, having any kind of shape, rounded or irregular, forming discrete mass of a composition different from the surrounding sediment.

Conformable strata / rocks — Said of a geological formation that is deposited in a continuous sequence, and has the same direction of stratification.

Conglomerate — Sedimentary rock composed of rounded *pebbles of pre-existing rocks and embedded in a fine-grained *matrix of *sand and *silt.

Conifer — A gymnosperm plant having needle-like or scale-like leaves and naked seeds contained in cones; they include pines, firs, and spruces.

Conjugate — Any geological feature that occurs in a pair, or in two sets, such as *joints, *folds, etc.

Conodont — Small fossils tooth-like in form of uncertain affinity, found in the Late *Precambrian to the Upper *Triassic.

Conrad Discontinuity — A seismically detectable boundary of discontinuity within the Earth's continental *crust, separating it into a lower basic layer and an upper granitic layer that is equivalent to the boundary between the *sial and the *sima. Beneath the ocean floors the upper layer is missing.

Continental Drift — A theory that proposes that the present positions of the continents and oceans resulted from the breaking up of a large single land mass or supercontinent of *Pangaea, about 200 million years ago, into *Gondwanaland in the south and *Laurasia in the north.

Contour — Lines on a map that connect points of elevation of the land surface of equal value with reference to a fixed point or datum, generally the mean sea level.

Convolute bedding — A deformation structure confined within a *clastic bed made up of thin intricately crumpled, twisted or folded *laminae.

Coprolite — A large-sized fossilized excrement of a vertebrate, ovoid or elongated in form, with surface marked by annular convolutions, often composed largely of calcium phosphate.

Coral — A hard calcareous substance secreted by certain colonial marine animals (*Anthozoa or rarely by *Hydrozoa polyps) as an external skeleton, typically forming large *reefs.

Core, Earth's — The central part of the Earth, below the **Mantle**, about 6900 km in thickness, having high density and probably consisting of nickel-iron.

Corona — The zone of concentric growth of a mineral around another mineral; it is generally applied to *reaction rims, *corrosion rims, and originally crystallized minerals.

Corrasion — Process which causes the mechanical renewal of rocks and soils by abrasive action or attrition like friction and impact of solid materials moved by running water, wind, waves, glaciers, etc. It is different from **Corrosion.**

Correlation — The correspondence in character and in stratigraphic position between geographically separated stratigraphic sections or rock bodies.

Corrosion — The process of *erosion by which rocks and soils are worn away and removed by natural chemical processes working on the surface of the Earth. It is different from **Corrasion.**

Corrosion rim — An outer border of one or more secondary minerals around an original crystal that is formed due to the corrosive action of its *magma.

Corundum — A very hard mineral, composition Al_2O_3; trigonal; pyramidal; hardness 9; sp. gr. 4; its transparent and variously coloured crystals are used as gemstones, like *ruby (red) and *sapphire (blue): refractive index 1.76/1.77–1.77/1.78; birefringence 0.008; dispersion 0.018.

Coset — A group of two or more units of strata or cross-bedding which show a uniform direction of current flow.

Country rock — A broad term for a preexisting rock body into which a mass of igneous rock(s) or mineral vein has intruded. Not to be confused with **Bedrock**.

Crater — (1) The funnel-shape hollow at the top of volcanic cone. (2) The hollow caused by the fall of a *meteorite on the Earth's surface.

Craton (Kraton) — A part of the Earth's crust that is relatively stable and is unaffected by orogenic activity.

Crenulation — Irregular or wavy small-scale folding or kinking.

Cretaceous — The topmost system/period of the *Mesozoic, lasting from about 145.5 to about 65.5 Ma ago. It is divided into two series / epochs. It was characterized by the emergence of flowering plants and the dominance and extinction of *dinosaurs. It was also a period of marine transgression, formation of swamps and massive alluvial deposits. *Gondwanaland broke up into South America, Africa, India, Africa and Antarctica. During this time turtles, rays and now common fish appeared; flowering plants were established.

Cretaceous-Tertiary (K-T) boundary — The end of the *Mesozoic when there was a mass extinction event that saw the end of *dinosaurs. It marks an important event in geologic history.

Crinoidea / Crinoids — A large class of primitive marine invertebrate animals (of phylum *Echinodermata) having a cup-shaped body enclosed by calcareous plates, with five or more feathery arms and typically attached to the sea bed by a long stalk. They are found from the *Ordovician to the present.

Cross-bedding — The development of internal laminations within a stratum at an inclined or oblique angle to the main bedding planes, caused by changes in the direction of water or wind currents during deposition. A cross-bedded unit usually consists of three elements: an upper layer of laminations parallel to the bedding plane called *topset, followed by inclined laminations called the *foreset, and underlain by laminations again parallel to the main bedding called the *bottomset. *Syn.* **Current bedding; False bedding.**

Crosscut — A mine working driven horizontally and at right angles to an *adit, *drift or *level.

Crude — Said of a petroleum product which is in a natural state and not yet processed or refined.

Crust, Earth's — The outermost portion of the Earth, lying above the *Moho, about 8–40 km in thickness, and composed largely of igneous rocks; it consists of two layers, the upper, discontinuous *Sial and the lower, continuous *Sima. Composition of the Crust: Oxygen (46.6%), Silicon (27.72%), Aluminium (8.13%), Iron (5.0%), Calcium (3.63%), Sodium (2.83%), Potassium (2.59%), Magnesium (2.09%) and other elements (1.41%).

Crustacea / Crustaceans — A large group of mainly aquatic *arthropods, that have a chitinous or calcareous exoskeleton, a pair of often much modified appendages on each segment and two pairs of antennae on the head. The group includes crabs, lobsters, shrimps, woodlice and barnacles. They have a wide range from the *Cambrian to the present.

Cryogenian — The middle *geochronometric subdivision of the *Neoproterozoic dated between 850 and 630 Ma ago, and lying above the *Tonian and below the *Ediacaran.

Cryptocrystalline — A rock having a crystalline structure visible only when magnified.

Cryptozoic — That part of the geologic time represented by rocks in which evidence of life is only slight and of primitive forms; *the Precambrian. *Cf.* **Azoic; Archaeozoic.**

Cryptozoon — A hemispherical or cabbage-like algal structure of variable size composed of irregular and concentric *laminae of variable thickness.

Crystal — A solid body made up of a chemical element, compound, or isomorphous mixture that has a regular repeating atomic structure that may be outwardly expressed by plane faces which have a natural geometrically regular form with symmetrically arranged plane faces.

Crystal classes — The 32 possible crystallographic combinations of the non-transitional elements of the outward symmetry of crystals.

Crystal faces — Planar faces bounding a crystal. These are: *pinacoid, *prism, *dome, and *pyramid.

Crystal forms — (1) The geometric shape of a crystal. (2) An assemblage of symmetrically equivalent crystal faces.

Crystal habit — (1) The general shape of a crystal, such as cubic, prismatic, pyramidal, fibrous. (2) The relative development of individual crystal forms and faces.

Crystal systems — Six groups of crystals classified on the basis of the symmetry of their crystal faces. These are *cubic or isometric, *tetragonal, *orthorhombic, *hexagonal, *monoclinic, and *triclinic. The hexagonal system includes the *trigonal system, which makes for seven crystal systems according to some authorities. Between the six systems, there is a total of 32 classes of symmetry.

Crystalline rocks / Crystallines — Rocks formed by the action of crystallization; an informal term that encompasses both igneous and metamorphic rocks.

Crystallite — A general term for a minute form of unknown mineralogical composition that may represent the initial stages of crystallization of a magma or glass.

Crystalloblastic — A typical metamorphic texture produced by recrystallisation under conditions of high viscosity and direct pressure.

Crystallographic axes — Certain imaginary fixed lines of reference of indefinite length extending in definite directions and intersecting at the center of the crystal. They are three in number, except in the hexagonal system where they are four.

Cubic system — A crystal system characterized by three axes mutually at right angles and of equal length. It consists of five crystal classes. *Syn.* **Isometric System.**

Cuesta — A landform created by gently inclined harder strata that create a dip slope on one side and terminate with a steep slope or scarp on the other, forming capping over softer rocks.

Cuprite — A reddish copper ore mineral, Cu_2O; cubic; octahedral; massive / earthy; hardness 3.5–4; sp. gr. 6.

Current bedding — *Syn.* of **Cross bedding.**

Current lineation — *Syn.* of **Parting lineation.**

Cycad — A tall, palm-like plant (*gymnosperm) having compound leaves, and naked seeds in simple cones. They range from the *Permian to the present day.

Cyclothem — A series of sedimentary beds deposited as part of a single sedimentary cycle. They occur in repetitive sequences.

D

Daughter element — An element produced by the radioactive decay of a pre-existing element.

Decay constant — The probability of the decay of an atomic nucleus per unit time that characterizes a radioactive isotope. *Syn.* Disintegration constant; *See* also **Half life.**

Declination — The horizontal angle between *true north and *magnetic north at any given location on the Earth's surface.

Décollement — The plane marking the boundary between two different types of deformation in which the overlying rocks are generally deformed whereas the underlying ones may be unaffected. This is caused by the upper rock series sliding over the lower during folding.

Decomposition — The process of *weathering that changes rocks and minerals into new chemical or mineralogical combinations by chemical reactions.

Deformation — Any change or distortion in the attitude, shape or dimensions of a bed or layer after its formation due to folding, faulting, development of scistocity, and other features produced by tectonic forces.

Degradation — (1) The break down of rocks due to chemical action. (2) The lowering of a stream bed due to factors like scouring.

Delta — A fan-shaped, triangular tract of alluvial sediments formed at the mouth of a river opening on the sea in which there is a system of criss-crossing distributaries of the main river.

Dendrite — (1) A crystalline mass with a branching, tree-like structure, (2) A natural tree-like marking on a rock surface.

Denudation — The sum total of the processes of *weathering, *mass wasting, *transportation and *erosion that cause the progressive wearing away and lowering of the Earth's surface.

Deposit — (1) In sedimentology, an accumulation of sediments by water, wind, ice, or any other agency. (2) In economic geology, an accumulation by any agency of ore or other valuable Earth material.

Desiccation cracks — *See* **Mud cracks.**

Detrital — Formed from or pertaining to detritus; said especially of sediments, minerals, and rocks.

Detritus — Loose rock debris or mineral waste produce by the breaking, disintegration or wearing away of Earth's surfaces.

Devonian — The *Paleozoic system/period between the *Silurian and the *Carboniferous, extending from about 416.0 to about 359.2 Ma ago. It is divided into three series / epochs. It has the oldest continental deposits as well as extensive marine sediments containing fossils of armoured fish, *corals, *ammonites and *mollusks; first *amphibians and insects appeared, as also the first terrestrial leafy plants.

Diabase — It sometimes is used as synonym for *dolerite, but is an ambiguous term because it is defined differently in different countries.

Diablastic — A metamorphic rock texture consisting of acicular or fibrous minerals oriented in the same direction and intimately interpenetrated.

Diachronism — The occurrence of a feature or phenomenon in different geological periods.

Diagenesis — The process of physical and chemical changes that occur during the conversion or lithification of a sediment into a sedimentary rock.

Diamictite — A non-sorted or poorly sorted, non-calcareous sedimentary rock that contains a wide range of particle sizes ranging from *clay to *boulder size.

Diamond — A native crystalline form of carbon; cubic; octahedron; hardness 10; sp. gr. 3.5; refractive index 2.417; dispersion 0.044. It is dimorphous with *graphite.

Diaphthoresis — A type of metamorphism by which metamorphic minerals of a lower grade are formed at the cost of minerals characteristic of a higher grade of metamorphism, such as by lowering of temperatures. *Syn.* **Retrograde metamorphism.**

Diapir — A domed rock formation in which the plastic core of the rock has squeezed upward to pierce the overlying strata.

Diastem — A break in sedimentation of very short duration as shown by an erosional contact between two rock sequences.

Diastrophism — The disturbance and dislocation of the Earth's crust, including bending, folding and breaking that results in major inequalities of its surface.

Diatom — Any of a class of minute planktonic unicellular or colonial *algae with silicified skeletons, occurring in both marine and freshwater.

Diatomite — (1) A fine-grained sedimentary rock formed from consolidated diatomeaceous earth. (2) A light, friable siliceous material derived from *diatom remains and used especially as a mild abrasive.

Diatreme — A breccia-filled volcanic vertical pipe, plug or vent that usually results due to gaseous explosion of the magma on its way up through the overlying strata, such as a *kimberlite *pipe.

Dinosaurs — A diverse group of fossil *reptiles that dominated life on the land for 140 million years from the late *Triassic until their extinction at the end of the *Cretaceous 65 million years ago, mostly in the *Mesozoic. Dinosaurs are distinguished from other reptiles by the way they stood with their limbs held vertically beneath their bodies rather than sticking out sideways. There are various theories how and why they suddenly disappeared, and the most accepted theory is that they were wiped out by the impact of a *meteorite.

Diopside — A green to white *pyroxene mineral, $CaMg(SiO_3)_2$; monoclinic; prismatic; hardness 6; sp. gr. 3.3.

Diorite — A coarse-grained *plutonic igneous rock containing less than 5% quartz, essentially containing more than 90 per cent *plagioclase, and one or more *ferromagnesian minerals.

Dip — The maximum angle, a stratum makes with the horizontal plane in a direction perpendicular to the **Strike** of the bedding plane of a stratified rock or any other planar surface.

Dip, Magnetic — The angle formed with the horizon by a magnetic needle free to rotate in the vertical plane.

Disconformity — When rock strata are essentially conformable (that is, they have the same dip) but are separated by changes of sediment type, and the older bed has an irregular or uneven surface or relief due to a long period of erosion or nondeposition.

Discontinuity — *See* **Conrad Discontinuity**, **Gutenberg Discontinuity** and **Mohorovičić Discontinuity**.

Discordance — The cross-cutting relationship of an igneous rock body with bedding or foliation.

Disintegration — Mechanical *weathering of rocks by natural processes.

Disthene — *Syn.* of **Kyanite.**

Division — A principal taxonomic category in botany that ranks above class and below kingdom, equivalent to the *phylum in zoology.

Dogger — Middle part of the *Jurassic, corresponding roughly with the standard Middle. *Jurassic, above the *Lias and below the *Malm, extending from 178.0 to 157.1 Ma (GTS). According to ICS-2004, the middle Jurassic ranges from 175.6 $\pm$ 2.0 to 161.2 $\pm$ 4.0 Ma.

Dolerite — A medium-grained basic *hypabyssal igneous rock, mineralogically of the same composition as *gabbro and *basalt, often occurring as *dykes, *sills and *plugs. *Cf.* **Diabase.**

Dolomite — (1) White carbonate mineral, composition $CaMg(CO_3)_2$; trigonal, rhombohedral crystals common; frequently massive; hardness 3.5–4; sp. gr. 2.85. (2) A carbonate rock composed of a high ratio of magnesium to calcium carbonate.

Dome — (1) A rounded uplifted landform or rock mass. (2) A large magmatic or **migmatitic** intrusion whose surface is convex upward and whose sides slope away at low but gradually increasing angles. (3) An uplift or anticlinal structure, circular or elliptical in outline, in which the rocks dip gently away in all directions. (4) An open crystal form whose faces are parallel to the vertical axis but meet both the horizontal axes.

Double refraction — *Syn.* of **Birefriengence.**

Downthrow — The amount of the downward vertical displacement of a fault block relative to the other.

Drift — (1) Any rock material (clay, silt, sand, shingle, gravel, boulders, or any combination of these) transported or deposited by wind (*loess), waves or currents (coastal or *littoral drift) or a glacier (glacial drift). (2) A nearly horizontal mine passageway driven on or parallel to the course of a vein or rock stratum.

Drive — A tunnel for mining driven along or near an ore body.

Dross — (1) Scum on formed on the surface of molten metal. (2) Inferior or worthless coal.

Drumlin — An oval mound or small hill consisting of compacted boulder clay formed by glacial action.

Druse — A rock cavity lined with a crust of projecting crystals.

Ductile — Capable of being drawn out or hammered into thin strips or wire.

Dune, Sand — *See* **Sand Dune**.

Dunite — An ultrabasic *plutonic igneous rock composed almost entirely of *olivine.

Durain — A coal material that is dull, has matte lustre, and is grey to brownish in colour with granular fracture.

Dyke — A sheet-like vertical or subvertical intrusion of igneous rock cutting across existing *country rock.

Dynamical geology — A general term for the branch of geology that deals with the causes and processes of geological phenomena. *Syn.* **Physical Geology.**

E

Early — The qualifier is applied to the name of a geologic-time unit (Period, Epoch) to indicate relative time designation and corresponds to *Lower as applied to the name of the equivalent *chronostratigraphic unit (System, Series).

Earth — The planet third from the sun at the maximum distance of 152.6 million km and the minimum distance of 147.4 million km; age about 4.6 billion years.

Earth science(s) — Sciences dealing with the Earth or one or more of its parts, such as geology, meterorology, glaciology and oceanography, as also the origin of the Earth and the solar system.

Earthquake — A sudden violent shaking or trembling of the ground as a result of movements within the Earth's crust that is tectonic or volcanic in origin. It is measured for its **Intensity** and its **Magnitude** (*See* **Richter Scale**).

Earthquake epicenter — The point on the Earth's surface vertically above the *focus of an earthquake.

Earthquake focus (Pl. **Foci / Focuses)** — The point of origin of an earthquake below the Earth's surface. *Syn.* **Hypocentre.**

Echinodermata / Echinoderms — A large marine invertebrate phylum characterized by its typically radial symmetry; body enclosed by a variety of calcareous plates, ossicles and spines. They range from the *Cambrian to the present.

Eclogite — A coarse-grained granular metamorphic rock consisting essentially of bright green omphacite *pyroxene and deep red alamandine-pyrope *garnet.

Economic geology — The branch of geology that deals with the exploration and exploitation of minerals for profit.

Ectasian — The middle *geochronometric subdivision of the *Mesoproterozoic dated between 1400 and 1200 Ma ago, and occurring above the *Calymmian and below the *Stenian.

Ediacaran — The upper *geochronometric subdivision of the *Neoproterozoic dated between 630 and 542 Ma ago. This system/period marks the end of the *Proterozoic (and the *Precambrian), and lies below the *Cambrian (at the start of the *Phanerozoic).

Ediacaran fauna — Term applied to soft-bodied fossil remains dating from the late Neoproterozoic interval of time.

Effervescence — The phenomenon of bubbling, hissing, and foaming when gas escapes from a carbonate mineral when dilute hydrochloric acid is applied on its surface.

Element — Any of more than 100 fundamental substances that consist of atoms of only one kind with the same atomic number.

Eluvial deposit — A deposit formed from the disintegration or decomposition of the original host rock close to it.

Eluvium — A weathered material, *float, or residue resulting from disintegration or decomposition of rock which is still at, or near, its place of formation. *Cf.* **Alluvium.**

Emerald — A gem variety of **Beryl;** refractive index 1.568–1.602/1.568–1.6025; birefringence 0.005–0.009; dispersion 0.014.

Emery — A grayish black form of *corundum containing *magnetite, used in powdered form as an *abrasive.

Emplacement — (1) Deposition of an ore mineral in a host body. (2) Process or development of a body of igneous rock within another rock body.

Enclave — *Syn.* of **Xenolith.**

Endogenic / Endogenetic — Formed or occurring beneath the surface of the Earth.

Engineering geology — A discipline which is concerned with the application of geological knowledge for the location, design and construction of engineering works.

Enrichment — (1) The process by which the relative amount of one constituent mineral contained in a deposit is enhanced. (2) The process of increment of a particular isotope of an element, especially that of a fissile isotope.

Enstatite — *See* **Hypersthene.**

Environmental geology — A branch of geology that deals with Earth processes, Earth resources and engineering properties of Earth materials that are relevant to the protection of the natural ecosystems.

Eoarchean — The lowermost erathem / era of the *Archaean, suggested by ICS-2004. It lies under the *Paleoarchean (base 3600 Ma), but the lowe limit is not defined though it may be considered at 3850 Ma on the basis of the oldest preserved *supracrustals.

Eocambrian — An informal name for the late Precambrian, roughly equivalent to the *Riphean.

Eocene — The middle series/epoch of the three-fold *Palaeogene system/period, lasting from about 55.8 Ma ago to about 33.9 Ma ago, lying above the *Palaeocene and below the *Oligocene. Traditionally, it formed the second oldest series/epoch of the five-fold *Tertiary, not recognized now by IUGS as a formal stratigraphic unit. During this time mountain formation continued and glaciers became common in the high mountain ranges. Greenland and Australia separated. It was characterized by a warmer climate and the appearance of the modern flora and fauna, when large tropical jungles appeared and mammals were established.

Eon (Aeon) — The formal *geochronologic division of geologic time ranking above an *Era. *See* **Eonothem.**

Eonothem — The formal *chronostratigraphic unit of the highest rank, corresponding to the body of rocks formed during the time span of an *Eon, and ranking above *Erathems/*Eras. Two Eonothems/eras were recognized originally, *viz.,* the *Precambrian or *Azoic and the *Phanerozoic. According to the latest proposal of ICS-2004, there are four erathems/eons, viz., *Hadean, *Archaean, *Proterozoic, and *Phanerozoic. The International Stratigraphic Charts of ICS show the *Precambrian without a rank designation.

Eozic — An obsolete term for a division of the *Precambrian that follows the Archaeozic and the * Proterozoic.

Epeirogenesis / Epeirogeney — Large scale changes in the level of the Earth's crust in which the surface of the continents have been simply elevated or depressed, with little or no folding; it is a process of continent building.

Epicentre of earthquake — The point on the Earth's surface vertically above the **Focus** of an earthquake.

Epidote — A typically green, rock-forming group of orthosilicate minerals, orthorhombic (zoisite) and monoclinic (epidote, clinozoisite, piedmontite, allanite); massive/granular; hardness 6–7 ; sp. gr. about 3.4.

Epigenesis — A process occurring at or near the surface of the Earth.

Epithermal deposit — A *hydrothermal mineral deposit formed at low temperatures (50°–200°C) near the surface of the Earth (within about 1.5 km), generally as veins.

Epoch — *See* **Series**.

Era — *See* **Erathem**.

Erathem — This chronostratigraphic term is one rank below *Eonothem; it is used for a group of *Systems, and its geochronologic (time) equivalent is called an *Era which is made up of equivalent *Periods. Both take the same name, consisting of the *Paleozoic (old life), the *Mesozoic (the middle life) and the *Cenozoic (new life) in the *Phanerozoic, while there are three erathem/eras in the *Proterozoic (Paleoproterozoic, Mesoproterozoic, and Neoproterozoic) and four in the *Archaean (Eoarchean, Paleoarchean, Mesoarchean, and Neoarchean).

Erosion — The process of destruction caused by the action of wind, water, ice, or any other agency that wears away the land surface.

Erratic/Erratic block — A rock body carried by glacial ice or by floating ice deposited at some distance from the outcrop from which it was derived, and generally, but not necessarily, resting on bedrock of a different kind.

Escarpment — Same as **Scarp.**

Esker / Osar — A long ridge of gravel, boulders and other loose material deposited by melt water from a retreating glacier or ice sheet.

Essential mineral — A mineral constituent of a rock that is necessary to its classification and nomenclature, but that is not necessarily present in large amounts. *Cf.* **Accessory minerals.**

Estuary — The funnel-shaped tidal mouth of a large river where fresh water comes into contact with sea water.

Eugeosyncline — A geosyncline in which there is an accumulation of thick sediments with an abundance of volcanic rocks forming some distance from the *craton.

Euhedral — Said of a mineral crystal having faces corresponding to its regular crystal form. *Syn* : **Idiomorphic; Automorphic.**

Eurypterida — A group of usually large-sized *arthropods resembling large scorpions. They ranged from the *Ordovician to *Permian.

Eustasy — A condition of world-wide sea level changes or fluctuations that may be caused by several types of changes.

Euxinic — (1) Concerning a marine environment of restricted circulation and stagnation or anaerobic conditions (deficient in oxygen). (2) Pertaining to a rock facies that includes black shales and graphitic sediments of various kinds.

Evaporites — Sedimentary deposits formed in an enclosed basin by the precipitation and evaporation of dissolved salts, such as *halite and *gypsum.

Exfoliation — A process of weathering which results in the peeling of thin layers of rock from the surface.

Exogenic — Said of a process or event that occurs on or near the surface of the Earth.

Exotic block — A body of rock occurring in a lithologic association foreign to that in which it was formed.

Expanding Earth — A model suggesting that the Earth expanded significantly over geological time that resulted in the movement of continents.

Exploitation — Act of making productive use of and deriving benefit from a mineral deposit by working it.

Exploration — The act of investigation, study, evaluation and analysis of any geological activity, particularly relating to discovering mineral deposits.

Exposure — A part of a rock formation or geologic structure that is visible either naturally or artificially on the surface.

Extinction angle — The angle through which a thin section of a *birefringent mineral must be rotated from a known crystallographic plane to a position at which it gives the maximum darkness under a polarizing microscope.

Extrusive rocks — Rocks that have been erupted on the surface of the Earth. They include *volcanic and *pyroclastic rocks.

F

Fabric — (1) The orientation, or its absence, of discrete particles, crystals, or cement of which a sedimentary rock is composed. (2) The entire configuration of all those components that make up a deformed rock, be they spatial or geometrical.

Face — (1) An exposed, vertical or sloping surface of a hill or rock slope. (2) Planar faces bounding a crystal. These are: *pinacoid, *prism, *dome, and * pyramid.

Facies — According to the International Stratigraphic Guide the term 'facies' originally meant the lateral change in lithologic aspect of a stratigraphic unit. It meaning has now been broadened to express a wide range of geologic concepts : environment of deposition, lithologic composition, geographic, climatic or tectonic association, etc.

Faecal (Fecal) pellet — A mineralized excreta, mainly of invertebrates, in the form of minute ovoids, and rarely rod-shaped, composed of silt and mud and devoid of internal structure.

False bedding — *Syn.* of **Cross bedding.**

Fanglomerate — A rudaceous rock consisting of variously-sized fragments deposited in an alluvial fan and cemented to form a rock body.

Fault — An extended break or fracture in a rock formation in the Earth's crust accompanied by the relative displacement and discontinuity of strata. The dip of a *fault plane is the angle which it makes with the horizontal surface. The strike of a fault plane is the direction a right angle to the line of dip.

Fault, Dip — A type of fault that strikes parallel with the dip of the affected beds.

Fault, Hinge — A fault whose displacement decreases from the maximum to zero along the strike; the end acts as a hinge.

Fault, Normal — A fault with dominant component of dip-slip displacement, and the *hanging wall displaced downwards relative to the *footwall.

Fault, Oblique — This type of fault trends away from the vertical or is oblique to the strike of the constituent rocks or the dominant structure.

Fault, Reverse — A fault with a major dip-slip component in which the *hanging wall is displaced on the up throw side relative to the down throw side.

Fault, Step — A series of closely spaced faults, all downthrown in the same direction.

Fault, Strike — A type of fault that trends parallel to the strike of the strata concerned.

Fault, Strike-slip — A fault where the movement is parallel to the fault strike. *Tear fault, or *Wrench fault are similar.

Fault, Tear — A steep fault in which the block movement is essentially horizontal or low angle. This type of fault could be dextral or sinistral, that is, the outcrops on the opposite side of the fault plane are displaced to the right or left. *Syn.* *Wrench fault, and similar to *Strike-slip fault.

Fault, Transcurrent — A large-scale *strike-slip fault in which the fault surface is steeply inclined. *Syn.* **Transverse thrust**.

Fault, Wrench — *Syn.* of **Tear fault.**

Fault block — A body of rock differing in elevation from its surroundings due to faulting.

Fault breccia — A non-foliated *breccia composed of angular fragments formed due to crushing, shattering or shearing of rocks during movement of a fault.

Fault plane — A fault surface which is more or less planar.

Fauna — Collective term for all animal population of a region, habitat or geological period.

Feldspars — A group of aluminium silicate minerals containing various proportions of potassium, sodium and calcium. *Orthoclase and *microcline (both $KAlSi_3O_8$) are called *alkali or potash / potassium feldspars; the Albite ($NaAlSi_3O_8$)-

Anorthite ($CaAl_2Si_2O_8$) series is known as *plagioclase or *soda-lime / soda calcium feldspars. They are an important group of rock-forming minerals and constitute about half of the rocks of the Earth's crust.

Feldspathoids — A group of rock-forming silicate minerals characterized by three-dimensional silicate lattices (tectosilicates), that contain Na and/or K. They are *unsaturated, i.e., they can never occur in association with free quartz. They occur mostly in cubic or hexagonal systems. The simple feldspathoids have different degrees of undersaturation, and are white or colourless and hexagonal : (i) the nepheline-kalsilite series based on ($AlSiO_4$); and (ii) leucite-analcite series based on ($AlSi_2O_6$). Complex feldspathoids occur in two groups: (i) sodalite group is cubic, and (ii) cancrinite group is hexagonal.

Felsic — Relating to or denoting a group of light-coloured minerals, including feldspar, quartz and muscovite.

Felsite — A fine, evenly-grained acid or intermediate igneous rock forming *dykes and *veins both in the country rocks and in the parent plutonic mass.

Felsitic — A *microcrystalline to *cryptocrystalline texture of fine-grained *extrusive igneous rocks.

Femic — Denoting the iron- and magnesium-rich minerals of the *CIPW normative classification.

Fenster — *Syn.* of **Window.**

Ferromagnesian minerals — Minerals that are rich in iron and/or magnesium and are usually dark in colour, such as *pyroxenes, *amphiboles, *olivines and *biotite.

Ferruginous — Said of any rock in which iron oxide is present in the form of cement or in any other manner, visible usually as red or rusty colour.

Festoon bedding — A type of *cross-bedding consisting of small, elongated troughs that are filled with sets of thin laminae.

Fibroblastic — A *homoblastic type of metamorphic texture produced by development during crystallization of fibrous minerals.

Filiform — Slender and long thread-like crystals.

Fireclay — A kaolinitic *argillite found associated with *coal seams which is high in Al_2O_3 and is capable of withstanding high temperatures, chiefly used for making refractory bricks to be used as furnace lining.

Firn — *Syn.* of **Névé.**

Fissility — The tendency of a rock, particularily a sedimentary rock, to split along surfaces parallel to the lamination planes.

Fission track dating — A method of absolute age dating based on measurement of fission tracks during decay of ^{238}U.

Fissure — A narrow, long crack in a rock body.

Flaser — A structure of metamorphic rock where granular minerals are arranged in streaks in the matrix.

Flint — A massive hard *chert (quartz) that produces a spark when struck by steel.

Float — A general term for a mass of displaced fragments of a rock occurring on a hillside below an outcropping ledge or *vein. The term is especially used for *eluvial minerals occurring in a *placer deposit.

Flora — Collective term for all plant population of a region, habitat or geological period.

Flow — (1) A body of fluid lava pouring out of a volcano. (2) A discrete extrusive volcanic body distinguished by texture, composition, or other criteria as a lithostratigraphic unit identified by a proper name.

Fludial — A fine-grained texture of lavas and other glassy igneous rocks characterized by elongated platy or prismatic mineral crystals oriented along planes of lamillar flowage as a result of slow motion.

Fluorescence — *Luminescence emitted by a substance when it is exposed to incident radiation of a shorter wavelength such as X-ray or ultraviolet light.

Fluorite / Fluorspar — A mineral with composition CaF_2; cubic; massive; hardness 4; sp. gr. 3.18; white and different colours.

Flute cast — Structure found in swarms prominently on the sole of *turbiditie sandstones consisting of a raised, oblong, and subconical bulge; it has a steep or blunt bulbous or beaked upcurrent end from which the structure flattens out in the downcurrent direction and merges with the bedding plane. It is formed by the filling of a flute in the underlying sediment.

Fluvial / Fluviatile — Concerning, found in, or produced by a river.

Fluvioglacial — Relating to or denoting erosion or deposition caused by flowing meltwater from *glaciers or *ice sheets.

Fly ash — Fine ash produced after burning of coal.

Flysch — Marine sedimentary *facies consisting of a thick sequence of thinly-bedded, graded argillaceous rocks and impure sandstones, rhythmeically interbedded with *greywackes and *conglomerate produced by erosion of uprising and developing fold structures.

Focus of earthquake — The point of origin of an earthquake; it is the source of the seismic waves produced during an earthquake.

Fold — The forms produced by bending or flexture of rocks after they were deposited or formed. A fold generally consists of two limbs with an axial plane in-between. A fold is said to *plunge if the axis is inclined, that is, it is not horizontal; the amount of plunge is the angle formed between the axis and the horizontal line lying in a common vertical plane. The *pitch or *rake of a fold is the angle between the horizontal and the axis measured on the axial plane. The *hinge line is the imaginary line along which a change in the amount and / or direction of maximum curvature at the crest of the fold is determined.

Fold, Asymmetrical — A fold in which the two limbs are differently inclined or have different dips about the axial plane.

Fold, Box — A fold with a rough rectangular cross-section on three sides.

Fold, Chevron — It is a fold in which the limbs are straight, generally of equal length, with sharp crests and several are packed together. *Syn.* Accordion fold; Concertina fold; Zig-zag fold.

Fold, Closed — In a fold like this the two limbs are closer at angles roughly between 30° and 70°.

Fold, Cross — A fold whose axis trends at an angle to the general fold in the region.

Fold, Open — In a fold like this, the two limbs open widely at inclinations greater than 70°.

Fold, Overturned — An inclined fold in which the two limbs tend to dip in the same direction at different amounts, that is when one limb is inverted.

Fold, Parallel — A type of fold in which the thickness of beds is constant everywhere perpendicular to the folded layer surface.

Fold, Ptygmatic — *See* **Ptygmatic folds.**

Fold, Recumbent — In a fold when the axial plane is horizontal or nearly so, and the two limbs seem to be riding on each other.

Fold, Symmetrical — In a fold when the two limbs are similarly inclined or dipping on both sides of the axial plane.

Fold, Tight — In this type of fold the two limbs are very close, almost touching each other.

Foliation — The structure in a metamorphic rock which is caused by parallel orientation of platy, layered or planar arrangement of minerals, and along which the rock can be split.

Footwall — The underlying side of a fault, ore body, or mine working, especially the wall rock beneath an inclined fault plane or vein.

Foraminifera / Foraminifers — An order of single-celled planktonic animal (*Protozoa) with a perforated chalky shell through which slender protrusions of protoplasm extend. They occur from the *Cambrian but are found extensively from the *Ordovician to the present.

Foredeep — An elongated depression bordering an *island arc or other *orogenic belt.

Foreland — A stable area of older cratonic rocks marginal to an orogenic belt, generally part of the continental crust.

Foreset — *See* **Cross bedding.**

Formation — The primary formal unit of *lithostratigraphic classification. It consists of a geographic place name followed by a lithologic term. If it consists of a mixed lithology, the term 'Formation' is used in place of the lithologic term. Both elements of the name are capitalized.

Form-line — Lines on a map to show relief similar to *contour lines but not accurately or instrumentally surveyed. They do not depict accurate surface elevations but only show the general surface slopes or configuration of the terrain. They are shown as broken lines to distinguish them from contours.

Fossil — (1) A usually mineralized remain or impression of a once living organism found in sedimentary rocks. The term is generally restricted to organisms that lived in geologic ages earlier to the last *Ice Age. Fossils typically comprise the bodies or parts of the organisms themselves, but also include a variety of *trace fossils. Fossils may be preserved in the following forms: (a) With unaltered hard parts such as calcitic shells and teeth. (b) With hard parts altered by petrification such that calcareous shells replaced with silica. (c) By infilling of pore spaces in shells, cellular plant material, or bones by different substances like silica, calcite, etc. (d) With altered soft parts by complete removal leaving an impression as by plants or fish. (e) Rarely with unaltered soft parts as in *amber. (2) Loosely for a geologically old material or feature.

Fossil, Derived — An organic remain removed from its original site in an older formation and then redeposited at a different locality in a younger formation.

Fossil, Index — A fossil species which by its abundance identifies and dates a specific horizon.

Fossil, Remanié — An organic body reworked from an older stratum and redeposited in a new stratum.

Fossil, Zone — A fossil characteristic of a particular horizon which is restricted in time.

Fossil fuel — Any of carbonaceous rocks or hydrocarbons used as fuel, such as *coal or *petroleum.

Fracture — The shape of the surface formed by a freshly broken mineral or rock when it is broken in a random direction other than that of a cleavage in crystalline minerals.

Fuller's earth — *See* **Montmorillonite**.

Fumarole — A hole in a volcanic region from which issue hot gases and vapour.

Fungi (Sing. **Fungus**) — A major group of saprophytic and parasitic spore-producing microscopic organism usually classified as plants that lack chlorophyll. They range from at least Late *Precambrian and continue today.

Furongian — The name given by ICS-2004 to the upper / late series/ epoch of the *Cambrian, about 501.0 to about 488.3 Ma.

Fusain — A *coal material which has silky luster, fibrous structure, is friable, and is black in colour.

G

Gabbro — A coarse-grained *plutonic igneous rock consisting of basic *plagioclase feldspars, *pyroxene and *olivine, with minor quartz and having *magnetite and *ilmenite as common accessories.

Gabbroid — A preliminary field term for a *plutonic igneous rock with less than 20 per cent quartz, less than 10 per cent *feldspar and with *pyroxene and *olivine forming the bulk.

Galena — The principal ore mineral of lead, PbS; cubic; massive; hardness 2.5; sp. gr. 7.5; metallic bluish grey in colour. Miner's term 'Lead-glance'.

Gall, Clay — A markedly flattened and somewhat rounded pellet, fragment or body of clay embedded in a sandy *matrix.

Gangue — The material of relatively small value or of no commercial value, surrounding or overlying a metallic **Ore** in a **Lode** or **Vein**; it is usually nonmetallic.

Ganister — A close-grained, hard, quartzose sandstone or quartzite used for making silica bricks for furnace lining.

Garnets — A group of silicate minerals of a variety of colours occurring mainly in metamorphic rocks but also found in *pegmatites. They have a structure consisting of independent SiO_4 tetrahedra and AlO_6 octahedra, which are linked by cations 8-coordination, where the divalent metals are magnesium, iron, manganese or calcium and the trivalent metals are : aluminium, iron or chromium. Important varieties are pyrope (Mg, Al), alamandine (Fe, Al), grossularite (Ca, Al), and andradite (Ca, Fe). Some transparent varieties are used as gemstones. They occur in cubic system; hardness 6.5–7.5 varying with composition; sp. gr. 3.15–4.3; high refractive index.

Gastrolith — A small stone found in the stomach of an animal, and sometimes found along with their fossil remains.

Gastropoda / Gastropods — A large class of marine, freshwater and terrestrial *Mollusca having a body contained in asymmetric helically coiled shell with apex pointing posteriorily away from head. They range from the Early *Cambrian to the present day; they have been used as zonal indices in the *Tertiary.

Geanticline — A very large anticlinal structure that has developed within geosynclinal sediments as a result of lateral compression.

Gem / Gemstone — A mineral or other natural material that has the necessary beauty and durability for personal adornment, that is, a precious or semi-precious mineral when cut and polished.

Gemology (Gemmology) — The scientific study of gemstones, including their classification and identification.

Genotype — The type species of a genus. Contrasted with **Phenotype.**

Genus (Pl. **Genera)** — A category in biological classification consisting of one or more closely related and morphologically similar species. The name of the genus and the species together form the scientific name of the organism printed in italics (*binomial nomenclature). The name of the genus is capitalized.

Geobotanical prospecting — The study of plant morphology and distribution as indicators of possible ore occurrences.

Geochemistry — Science dealing with the chemical composition of and chemical changes in the solid matter of the Earth (or a celestial body like the moon).

Geochron — (1) An interval of geologic time corresponding to a *lithostratigraphic unit. (2) Time during which the rocks of the corresponding stage or substage (*chronostratigraphic units) were formed.

Geochronologic units — A division of time traditionally distinguished on the basis of rock record as expressed by a *chronostratigraphic unit. The Geochronologic units in order of decreasing rank are given under the head **Chronostratigraphic units**. Their names are the same as corresponding chronostratigraphic units.

Geochronology — The branch of geology concerned with the measurements of time intervals on a geological scale and dating of rock formations and geological events.

Geochronometry — The branch of *geochronology that deals with the quantitative (numerical) measurement of geological time in thousands or millions of years.

Geode — A nodule of rock having a small cavity lined with crystals or mineral matter.

Geodesy — Branch of applied mathematics concerned with the determination of the size and shape of the Earth and the exact position of points on its surface with the description of variations of its gravity field.

Geography — Science dealing with the description , distribution and interaction of the diverse physical, biological and cultural features of the Earth's surface.

Geohydrology — Science dealing with the character, source and mode of occurrence of underground water.

Geoid — The surface within or around the Earth that is everywhere normal to the direction of gravity or coincides with mean sea level in the ocean. In simple words, it is used to signify the shape of the Earth taken at mean sea level.

Geologic column — A schematic diagram that shows in a single column the various beds and stratigraphic units of a given locality, area or region. For the purpose of the diagram the dips are adjusted to the horizontal.

Geologic map — A map, generally on the base of a topographic map, on which are recorded all surface informations about the distribution, boundaries, altitudes, etc., of all rock units.

Geologic section — Any sequence of rock units found in a region on the basis of a geologic map and/or subsurface information (from drill logs, mine shafts, etc.).

Geologic time — The long period of time occupied by the Earth's geologic history.

Geology — Science dealing with the history of the Earth and its life as recorded in its rock.

Geomagnetism — Branch of geology concerned with the magnetic properties of the Earth.

Geomorphology — Science dealing with the relief and physical features of the surface of the Earth and their relation to its geological structure.

Geophysical prospecting — The use of geophysical tools for prospecting for minerals and oil and gas, that involves both aerial and ground methods.

Geophysics — Science dealing with the physical processes and phenomena of the Earth.

Geoscience(s) — All the sciences dealing with the Earth, like geology, geophysics, geochemistry, oceanography, etc.

Geosynclines — Major downward flexures or depressions of the Earth's crust that gradually fill with sediments as floor subsides, resulting in the formation of an enormous thickness of sedimentary rocks. They are classified into following types : *Eugeosyncline; *Miogeosyncline; *Taphrogeosyncline; *Parageosyncline; *Zeugogeosyncline; *Autogeosyncline.

Geothermal — Relating to or produced by the internal heat of the Earth.

Geyser — A *hot spring which at regular intervals throws a jet of hot water and steam into the air.

Geyserite — A siliceous deposit produced around the mouth of a *hot spring or *geyser.

Ghat — (1) An Indian term for a mountain pass, or a path leading down a hill. (2) An Indian term for a river bank.

Glacier — A large body of compacted snow or ice moving slowly downslope on a mountain or valley or around the poles. Glaciers play considerable part in geomorphic processes.

Glaciology — The scientific study of ice in all its forms, including its crystal structure and physical properties, as well as *glaciers and *ice sheets in their geological context.

Glass — An amorphous rock or part of a rock that does not have discrete crystalline structure, formed by rapid cooling of a molten magmatic material.

Glass sand — An even-sized sand or friable sandstone consisting of almost pure quart (silica more than 95%) suitable for glass making. *Syn.* Silica sand.

Glauconite — A dull green earthy iron-potassium silicate mineral of the *mica group; monoclinic; hardness 2, sp. gr. 2.7.

Glaucophane — A mineral of the amphibole group; monoclinic; prismatic; hardness 6; sp. gr. 3.2.

Global Positioning System (GPS) — A system of constellation of artificial satellites orbiting 20,000 km above the Earth, moving on separate paths that allows three-dimensional positioning of location and height on the Earth's surface by the use of a receiving instrument.

Global tectonics — Tectonic processes related to large-scale movements of materials within the Earth on a global scale. *Cf.* **Plate tectonics; Expanding Earth.**

Gneiss — A fairly coarse-grained metamorphic rock consisting of quartz and feldspars with subordinate micas; *schistocity and banding are poor, irregular and discontinuous; it is formed by high-grade regional metamorphism.

Gondite — A metamorphic rock largely composed of quartz and serpentine, probably derived from manganese-bearing sediments.

Gondwanaland — The hypothetical southern supercontinent which began breaking up from the single mass of *Pangea about 200 million years ago due to *sea-floor spreading; it included Australia, Africa, Antarctica, India and South America.

Goniometer — An instrument, mechanical or optical, for the precise measurement of angles between crystal faces.

Gossan — An iron containing secondary deposit of oxides, typically yellowish or reddish, generally occurring above a sulphide ore deposit.

Graben — An elongated crustal unit or block that has been downthrown between two parallel faults relative to the surrounding area. When it forms a topographical trough it is called a **Rift valley.**

Grade — (1) In an ore or mineral deposit the relative quantity or the percentage of mineral or metal. *Syn.* **Tenor.** (2) In engineering geology, the degree of inclination with respect to the horizontal of a road, railway, embankment, or other engineering structure, expressed as a ratio of vertical to horizontal, or fraction such as metre / kilometre. (3) In coal classification based on quantity of inorganic material or ash left after burning.

Graded bedding — A type of sedimentation unit (mostly sandstone) in which each layer displays a gradual and progressive change in particle size, usually from coarse at the base fining towards the top. See also **Bouma cycle**.

Grain size, clastic rocks — The grain of a mineral that makes up a sedimentary rock is basic to the classification of *clastic rocks. The most widely used classification of grain size, modified from Wentworth, is given below:

Silt	< 1/16	mm
Very fine sand	1/16 – 1/8	mm
Fine sand	1/8 – 1/4	mm
Medium sand	1/4 – 1/2	mm
Coarse sand	1/2 – 1.0	mm
Very coarse sand	1.0 – 2.0	mm

Granite — A coarse-grained *plutonic igneous rock consisting essentially of 20–60% quartz, 10–65% alkali feldspar, and quite commonly small amount of *biotite and / or *muscovite *mica. Sometimes accessory minerals like : *apatite, *magnetite or *zircon may be present.

Granitization — The process or processes of metasomatic transformation of pre-existing rocks into granite due to action of granitic fluids arising from depth.

Granitoid — A IUGS preliminary field name for a granitic *plutonic *igneous rock with 20–60 per cent *quartz.

Granoblastic — A *homoblastic type of metamorphic texture in which platy grains are nearly equidimensional and are oriented at random in a non-schistose rock in which layering is not developed.

Granodiorite — A coarse-grained acidic plutonic igneous rock containing 20–60% quartz, 65–90% calc-alkali feldspar, and various *ferromagnesian minerals, mainly *hornblende and *biotite as accessories.

Granophyre — A granitic rock containing intergrown feldspar and quartz crystals.

Granophyric — Said of a texture of porphyritic igneous rocks made by interpenetration of *phenocrysts and the *groundmass.

Granule — (1) A small particle, especially part of a larger compact unit. (2) As a size term it is a particle between *sand and *pebble, 2–4 mm in diameter.

Granulite — A coarse, granular metamorphic rock (of sedimentary or igneous derivation) consisting mainly of feldspar and quartz composed of even-sized interlocking mineral grains, most of which do not show any preferred orientation but may show crude gneissic structure.

Graphic intergrowth — An intergrowth of alkali feldspar and quartz commonly found in granitic rocks and *pegmatites; the quartz is oriented along preferred directions within the feldspar.

Graphite — A soft, lustrous black or grey crystalline form of pure carbon; hexagonal; hardness 1; sp. gr. 2.1; good conductor of electricity. It is dimorphous with *diamond.

Graptolithina / Graptolites — Extinct planktonic marine invertebrate animals that lived in colonies; they had zooids in cups along a chitinous support. They ranged from the Middle *Cambrian to the *Carboniferous. They have considerable importance in biostratigraphy and are used as zone fossils throughout much of the *Silurian.

Gravel — A deposit of rounded stones, usually mixed with fine material such as clay or sand, formed by the action of water of a river, lake, or by the sea.

Gravity — The force that attracts a body towards the center of the Earth.

Gravity anomaly — The difference between the observed and the calculated force of gravity at a place due to the variation in density of the underlying rocks.

Greensands — Sedimentary rocks that are green in colour, the colour imparted by sufficient quantity of either *glauconite or *chlorite.

Greywacke (Graywacke) — A type of impure, coarse-grained sandstone composed of angular grains with lithic fragments set in a matrix of *clay, about 15%. *See* also **Turbidite.**

Grid — A network of two sets of uniformly-spaced parallel lines intersecting at right angles forming squares or rectangles, superimposed on a map, chart, or aerial photograph to permit precise identification, location and distance of a place or feature.

Grike (Gryke) — A fissure separating blocks of *clints in a limestone pavement.

Grit — Small, loose particles of stone or sand.

Groove cast — A small, rounded or sharp-crested rectilinear ridge produced on the sole of a sandstone by filling a groove or furrow made by some kind of a tool on the underlying soft sediment; they occur generally in sets.

Groundmass — The compact, fine-grained or glassy material in which the crystals are embedded in a porphyritic igneous rock. *Cf.* **Mesostasis.**

Groundwater — Water held underground in soil or in pores and crevices in rocks such as sandstones and limestones. *See* **Phreatic water.**

Group — A lithostratigraphic unit consisting of a succession of two or more contiguous or associated formations with significant and diagnostic lithologic properties in common. It is named after a geographical locality followed by the term 'Group'.

Grout — (1) The stony waste material of all sizes obtained in quarrying. (2) A cement slurry injected into spaces caused by fissures or openings to seal them.

Guadalupian — The middle series / epoch of the three-fold *Permian, extending from about 270.6 to about 260.4 Ma, lying over the *Cisuralian and the under the *Lopingian. It is composed of three stages.

Gutenberg Discontinuity — The seismic velocity discontinuity marking the boundary between the *mantle and the *core at 2900 km depth.

Gymnosperm — A plant of a group that comprises those that have seeds unprotected by an ovary or fruit, including **Conifers** and **Cycads**. Such plants first appeared in the Late Devonian and continue to the present.

Gypsum — A white mineral of hydrous sodium silicate ($CaSO_4.2H_2O$); monoclinic; tabular; hardness 2; sp. gr. 2.3.

H

Habit — (1) The typical appearance of an organism. (2) The relative development of individual crystal forms and faces.

Habitat — The natural home or environment of an organism where it naturally lives and grows.

Hachure — A series of short, straight, evenly-spaced parallel lines to show land relief on maps that are thick and plotted closer to each other for steep slopes, finer and somewhat wider-spaced for gentle slopes, but none at all for flat grounds.

Hade — It is the angle or dip that a fault or structural surface makes with the vertical; it is zero when the fault plane is vertical, and 90° when it is horizontal.

Hadean — The oldest era of the geochronometric classification of the *Precambrian according to GTS, starting presumably from the beginning of the Earth 4560 Ma ago to 3800 Ma ago.

Haematite (Hematite)—A red, earthy, important ore of iron, composition Fe_2O_3; trigonal; granular; hardness 5.5; sp.gr.4.9-5.3.

Half life — The time required for the radioactivity of an isotope to decrease to half of its original value. *See* also **Decay constant**.

Halite — A white, evaporite mineral of sodium chloride (NaCl); cubic; typically occurring as hopper-shaped crystals; hardness 2.5; sp. gr. 2.16. Also called **Rock salt** or simply **Salt**.

Hanging valley — A tributary valley that enters a main valley from a considerable height above the latter, so that a stream flowing down it enters the main valley in which a waterfall may develop.

Hanging wall — The overlying side of a fault, ore body, or mine working, especially the *wall rock above an inclined *fault plane or *vein.

Hardness — *See* **Mohs' Scale.**

Harpolith — A large sickle-shape igneous intrusion injected into previously deformed strata and subsequently deformed with the *country rock; it is essentially a *Phacolith with a vertical axis.

Heave — The measure of the horizontal component of the displacement between the upthrown and downthrown sides of a *fault.

Heavy minerals — Accessory minerals separated from a sedimentary rock that sink in bromoform (specific gravity 2.9). Included are *magnetite, *ilmenite, *zircon, *rutile, *kyanite, *garnet, *tourmaline, *sphene, *apatite, *biotite, *hornblende, *sphene.

Hemicrystalline — Said of a rock that is composed of both crystals and glass.

Hemihedral — Said of a class of a crystal system that has reduced symmetry, so that the general form has one half of the number of faces of the corresponding form in the **holohedral** class.

Hexagonal system — This crystal system has two divisions: hexagonal proper and *trigonal (or rhombohedral). Some authorities consider trigonal as a separate system, but here the two are considered as one, making a total of only six crystal systems. The hexagonal crystal system has four axes, three of which are equal and lie in the horizontal plane arranged mutually at 120°, while the fourth axis is vertical and has a shorter or longer length than the horizontal axis. In the hexagonal division there are four axial planes of symmetry; of these, three are like planes meeting at 60°. There are seven classes of symmetry in this division. In the trigonal division there are the same set of axes. However, there may be an alternative set of axes consisting of three nonorthogonal axes, equally inclined to the three-fold symmetry and making equal angles with each other. There are five classes of symmetry in this division.

Hiatus — A break in a stratigraphic sequence that may be due to erosion or nondeposition. It is a time missing between beds above and below an unconformity. It is supposed to be of a short duration.

Hinge line — *See* **Fold**.

Historical geology — A branch of geology that deals with investigations into *stratigraphy, *palaeontology and *geochronology together with the evolution of the Earth.

Holocene — According to ICS-2004, the most recent of the four-fold *Neogene, starting from 0.0115 Ma to the present. Earlier, ICS-2000 considered it as the upper series / epoch of the two-fold *Quaternary. During this time glaciers recede, sea level rises, forests flourish again, humans acquire agriculture and technology. *Syn.* **Recent.**

Holocrystalline — Said of an igneous rock made up essentially of crystalline minerals without any glass.

Holohedral — Said of a crystal which is completely developed and has all the faces.

Holohyaline — Said of an igneous rock that is essentially glassy.

Holotype — The single type specimen of a fossil species upon which the description and name of a new species is based.

Homeomorph — (1) An organism similar to another but derived from another ancestor. (2) A crystal similar to another crystal form and habit but with a different composition.

Hominidae / Homonids — A family of *Primates, including humans, their immediate ancestors and close extinct relatives. Two genera are usually recognized : **Australopithecus** and **Homo.** Hominid distinguishing features include truncal erectness, bipedality and rotary chewing.

Homoblastic — A type of *crystalloblastic metamorphic texture in which essential mineral constituents are of nearly equal size.

Homocline — A series of strata that have similar dip and strike, such as in a *monocline or isoclinal fold.

Homologous — Said of strata of the same general lithology in separated areas that are contemporaneous and can be correlated with each other.

Homotaxy (Homotaxis) — Taxonomic similarity between stratigraphic or fossil sequences in separate regions, or the condition of strata characterized by similar fossils occupying corresponding positions in different vertical sequences without connotation of similarity in age.

Horizon — An interface indicative of a particular position in a stratigraphic sequence. The type of horizon is indicated by a prefix, e.g., lithohorizon, biohorizon, chronohorizon.

Hornblende — An aluminous mineral of amphibole group; monoclinic; prismatic; hardness 5.5; sp. gr. 2.9–3.4.

Hornblendite — An igneous rock composed almost entirely of *hornblende.

Hornfel — A medium or fine-grained granulose metamorphic rock composed of nearly equidimensional grains without cleavage, schistosity or parallel arrangement of minerals, formed mainly by contact metamorphism of sediments.

Horst — An elongated block of rocks that has moved upwards relative to surrounding rocks due to faults on either side.

Hot spring — A stream of hot water issuing from the ground, often heated by the magma.

Hyaloclastic — A texture of volcanic rocks consisting of broken glass fragments formed by rapid cooling in water.

Hydrocarbons — Organic compounds of hydrogen and carbon, such as those that are the chief components of **Petroleum** and **Natural gas**.

Hydrogeology — The branch of geology that deals with subsurface waters and with related geological aspects of surface waters.

Hydrology — The branch of science concerned with the properties, distribution and circulation of water on or below the Earth's surface and in the atmosphere.

Hydrothermal — A term for any process associated with igneous activity which involves heated or superheated water.

Hydrothermal alteration — (1) The process of alteration of rocks or minerals by the reaction of hydrothermal water with pre-existing solid phase. (2) Serpentinisation of olivine and rhombic pyroxenes, chloritisation of ferromagnesian minerals, *saussuritisation of feldspars; kaolinisation of feldspars in granites.

Hydrothermal deposit — A mineral deposit formed by precipitation of *ore and *gangue minerals in rock openings or spaces by filling them from aqueous fluids at high temperatures and pressure.

Hydrozoa — A class of invertebrate animals belonging to the group *Coelenterata having simple and compound polyps. They range from the *Precambrian to Lower *Cambrian to the present.

Hypabyssal rocks — Medium-grained igneous rocks of occurring mainly as intrusives (*dykes and *sills) formed at intermediate depths.

Hypautomorphic — *See* **Hypidiomorphic**.

Hypersthene-Enstatite — A rock-forming mineral of the pyroxene group, $(Mg,Fe)SiO_3$; orthorhombic; massive; hardness 5.5; sp. gr. 3.5

Hypidiomorphic — A texture of igneous rocks formed by a mixture of *anhedral and *subhedral and/or *euhedral crystals. *Syn* : **Subautomorphic, Subidiomorphic** and **Hypautomorphic.**

Hypocentre — *Syn.* of **Earthquake focus.**

Hypocrystalline — Said of an igneous rock that is partly composed of glass along with crystals.

Hypothermal deposit — A *hydrothermal mineral deposit formed at great depths and in the temperature range of 300°–500°C.

Hypothesis (Pl. **Hypotheses)** — A tentative assumption, conception or proposition made on the basis of limited evidence as a starting point for further investigation. Hypothesis implies insufficient evidence to provide more than a tentative explanation. It is less firmly founded than a * Theory.

I

Ice — The solid state of water; it is a brittle transparent crystalline solid and plays an important part in the process of *weathering. Also *See* **Glacier.**

Ice Age — A period of time in the history of the Earth when *ice sheets and *glaciers advanced from polar regions to cover areas previously of temperate climate resulting in general lowering of temperatures. Several Ice Ages have been recorded in the geological past. The most recent Ice Age started about 1.8 million years ago and lasted until about 10,000 years ago in the *Pleistocene.

Ice cap — *Syn.* of **Ice sheet**.

Ice sheet — A cover of permanent ice and snow, specifically a *glacier forming an extensive area of relatively level land and flowing outward from its centre, especially in the polar region. *Syn.* **Ice cap.**

Iceland spar — A pure, transparent variety of calcite, showing strong double extinction, that is used for making *Nicol Prisms in a *polarizing microscope.

Ichnofossil — Same as **Trace fossil**.

Idioblastic — A typical *crystalloblastic metamorphic texture in which the essential mineral constituents are of nearly equal size.

Idiomorphic — *Syn.* of **Euhedral**.

Igneous rocks — Rocks that have solidified from molten *magma or *lava. They are classified into *plutonic, *hypabyssal, and *volcanic; sometimes *pyroclastic rocks are also included in the igneous class.

Ignimbrite — A volcanic rock formed by the consolidation of material deposited by *pyroclastic lava. *Syn.* **Welded Tuff.**

Illite — A *clay mineral group having essentially the crystal structure of *muscovite as it is derived from the alteration of *micas and *feldspars under alkaline conditions.

Ilmenite — A iron-black mineral that is ore of titanium, $FeTiO_3$; trigonal; sand grains; hardness 5.5; sp. gr. 4.7.

Imbricate structure — A series of minor thrust sheets all dipping in the same direction and lying lapped over each other in regular order.

Incertae sedis — A term applied to a fossil or modern specimen whose classification is regarded as uncertain.

Inclusion — A body or particle of distinct composition embedded in a rock or other material.

Index fossil — A fossil species whose abundance characterizes a specific stratigraphic horizon.

Induration — The process of heat, pressure, or the introduction of cementing material by which a rock gets hardened or is made more compact, such as a sediment getting turned into a sedimentary rock.

Industrial diamond — A diamond of inferior quality that cannot be used as a gem, and is used for drilling, cutting, polishing, etc.

Industrial mineral — A nonmetallic mineral or rock of economic value, other than metallic *ores, *mineral fuels and *gemstones.

Infracrustal — Said of the rocks that lie below the surface, but within the crust, and in general below the zone of *weathering and *diagenesis. *Cf.* **Supracrustal.**

Inlier — An area of exposed older rocks entirely surrounded by stratigraphically younger strata, usually resulting from erosion, folding or faulting. It is opposite of **Outlier.**

Inselberg — A prominent isolated hill-like rock feature rising abruptly from and surrounded by an extensive lowland. *Syn.* **Bornhardt.**

Intensity of Earthquake — A measure of the effects of an earthquake at a particular place depending upon its distance from the earthquake epicenter and the geology. It was first measured by a 10-degree scale called the *Rossi-Forel Scale, but was later replaced by another 10-degree scale devised by the Italian seismologist Giuseppi Mercalli, and later modified as a 12-degree scale called the *Modified Mercalli (MM) Scale on the criteria depending upon the duration and the number of tremors and their effect on humans and structures (the extent of damage). The MM Scale is now further modified as *MSK scale to take into consideration the type of structures affected.

In situ — The Latin term means 'in place', and is commonly used by the geologist to indicate rocks, minerals, fossils, etc., that occur in the same place and position where deposited or formed.

Interbedded — Said of a rock of a different type that occurs between two similar layers of strata or rock.

Interclast — A grain or particle of a different rock found embedded in a rock of different composition.

Interglacial — A period of warmer climatic conditions separating glacial phases of the *Pleistocene.

Intergrowth — Interlocking of grains of two different minerals resulting from their simultaneous crystallization.

Intermediate rocks — Igneous rocks that generally contain less than 10% quartz along with andesine-oligocene *plagioclase and/or alkali *feldspars; *feldspathoids may or may not be present (54–65% silica).

International Date Line — An arbitrary line through the Pacific Ocean approximately along the 180° meridian to designate the place where each calendar day begins; it deviates from the 180° longitude at places for adjustment of time between the continents of Asia and North America and in some of the islands.

Interstitial — Related to, or situated or occupying spaces or pores between rock grains.

Intrusion — A magmatic body that is emplaced in a pre-existing rock mass.

Intrusives / Intrusive rocks — Igneous rocks that occur as intrusions in the Earth's crust and have solidified beneath the surface, such as *dykes and *sills.

Invertebrate animals / Invertebrates — Animals that do not have a backbone, such as the *Arthropoda, *Coelenterata, and *Molluska.

Island arcs — Oceanic islands occurring in arc-shaped chains usually containing active *volcanoes and adjacent to deep-sea trenches. According to the Theory of *Plate Tectonics, island arcs are formed by volcanism generated when the rigid plates making up the Earth's surface are recycled into the Earth's interior beneath the trenches.

Isochron — A line on a diagram, chart or map connecting points at which an event occurs simultaneously or which represents the same time or time difference relating to the same time or equal times.

Iosocline — A fold whose limbs are parallel.

Isometric system — *Syn.* of **Cubic System.**

Isomorph — Similar in form, shape, or structure and relation, such as in crystals and fossils.

Isopach — A line that connects points of equal thickness of a geological stratum, formation, ore body, or a group of formations.

Isoseismal — A line on a map connecting places where an earthquake was experienced with equal *intensity.

Isostasy — A theory describing the state of equilibrium in the Earth's crust which can be considered as a large block floating on the semi-molten, denser material. Thus, high mountains must be regions where the crust is thickest with deep roots extending into the mantle.

Isotope — Any of two or more forms of the same chemical element, having the same atomic number, but different atomic mass or mass number and different physical properties.

Isotopic age — An age expressed in years or million of years calculated from the quantitative determination of the content of the parent and daughter nuclides during decay of radioactive elements.

J

Jade — A hard, tough, usually green stone consisting of two distinct minerals : *jadeite and *nephrite, valued for making ornaments and jewellery.

Jadeite — A green, blue or white *pyroxene, composition $NaAlSi_2O_6$; monoclinic; hardness 6.5–7; sp. gr. 3.35.

Jasper — A red, opaque variety of **chalcedony.**

Jaspilite — A rock consisting of alternating bands of *jasper and iron oxide; also called banded-haematie-jasper.

Java Man — The first known fossil of *Homo erectus*, found in Java in 1801. It was originally called *Pithecanthropus erectus*. Subsequent discoveries indicate trends of increased brain size and tooth reduction. Specimens date from about 0.8 to 0.3 Ma ago.

Joint — An opening or crack in the rock (generally competent rock) that forms the simplest fracture structure without displacement of the surface.

Jurassic — The middle division of the *Mesozoic, lying between the *Triassic and the *Cretaceous, extending from about 199.6 to about 145.5 Ma ago. It is divided into three series / epochs. During this time seas advanced, there was much river formation and high mountains got eroded. North America got separated from Africa. Central Atlantic began to open. It was characterized by dominant large reptiles (*dinosaurs) on land, sea and air with shallow seas rich in marine life, (e.g., *ammonites) and the appearance of the first birds and primitive *mammals, as also early flowers.

K

Kallar — An efflorescence formed over alluvial soils by carbonates, chlorides, sulphates, potassium and other salts brought up on the surface by capillary action. *Syn.* **Reh**.

Kankar (Kankur, Kunkur) — An Indian term for **Calcrete.**

Kaolinite — A group of clay minerals, the main constituent of china clay, mainly produced by the destruction of alkali feldspars under acidic conditions; composition $Al_4(Si_4O_{10})(OH)_8$; triclinic; hardness 2; sp. gr. 2.6.

Karst — An irregular landscape underlain by limestone which has been eroded by dissolution, producing fissures, caverns, sinkholes, etc.

Kelyphitic rim/border — A *corona structure consisting of a concentric shell or shells or a mineral often arranged in a radial or fibrous manner around a primary mineral. *Syn.* **Reaction rim.**

Keratophyres — Altered acid rocks associated with *spilites containing phenocrysts of sodi-potassic feldspars and *hornblende in a groundmass of albite, *chlorite, *epidote and quartz.

Kerogen — A solid organic material occurring in *shales and yielding oil when heated and distilled.

Khondalite — Light-coloured richly garnetiferous gneisses and schists characterized by an abundance of sillimanite and the presence of graphite.

Kimberlite — An ultramafic igneous rock containing at least 35% olivine, with one or more of the following in the groundmass monticellite, (*olivine), *phlogopite, *carbonates, *serpentine, *diopside. *Syn.* **Blue ground.**

Klippe (Pl. **klippen**) — A detached tectonic *outlier resulting from *erosion of a *thrust sheet, bounded below by a thrust plane, along with the constituent mass that has been moved often through an enormous distance from its place of origin.

Komatiite — An ultramafic volcanic rock composed mainly of *olivine and *pyroxene in a glassy devitrified *groundmass.

Kyanite — A blue thin-bladed mineral, Al_2SiO_5; triclinic; hardness 4 and 7 depending on direction; sp. gr. 3.63. It is trimorphous with **Andalusite** and **Sillimanite.** *Syn.* **Disthene.**

L

Labradolite — *See* **Plagioclase feldspars.**

Laccolith — A large mound or mass of igneous rock beneath the Earth's surface, caused by intrusion of magma between rock strata, producing a domical bulging in the overlying strata,

Lamellibranchiata / Lamellibranchs — A large class of aquatic *Mollusca with two hinged valve shells flattened from side to side. Range, Early *Cambrian to present day. *Syn.* **Pelecypoda; Bivalvia.**

Lamillar twinning — See **Twinning, Polysynthetic**.

Lamina (Pl. **Laminae / Laminas)** — *See* **Bed**.

Lamproite — Dark-coloured, *extrusive or *hypabyssal, potassium and magnesium-rich *mafic to *ultramafic alkaline *lamprophyre-type rock.

Lamprophyres — A group of medium-grained, dark-coloured, commonly porphyritic igneous rocks of intermediate composition containing a predominance of *ferromagnesian minerals, especially as *phenocrysts, associated with *feldspars and occasionally with *feldspathoid.

Landscape — All the visible features or landforms of an area.

Landslide — The downward movement of a large mass of earth or rock from a cliff or mountain.

Lapidary — A cutter, polisher, or engraver of precious stones, usually other than diamonds.

Lapidoblastic — A *homoblastic type metamorphic texture of *schists in which foliation or schistosity is produced by planar minerals, such as *micas.

Lapidolite — A colorless or pinkish lithium mica; monoclinic; hardness 2.5–4; sp. gr. 2.85.

Lapilli (singular, **Lapillus)** — Variously shaped round to angular fragments, 64–2 mm across, of lava thrown out during a volcanic eruption that may have solidified or be still viscous condition when ejected.

Late — The qualifier is applied to the name of a geologic-time unit (Period, Epoch) to indicate relative time designation and corresponds to *Upper as applied to the name of the equivalent time-stratigraphic unit (System, Series).

Lateral moraine — *See* **Moraine**.

Laterite — Tropical soil formed by weathering mainly of acidic rocks by concentration mostly of aluminium and iron oxides which give it the typical red or brown colour. On induration it becomes a hard rock.

Latitude — The angular distance of a place north or south of the equator which is zero degree (0°) of latitude. There are 90 degrees north of the equator (Northern Hemisphere), and 90 degrees on its south (Southern Hemisphere); they are imaginary approximate circles around the Earth, parallel to the equator.

Laurasia — The northern supercontinent comprising present-day North America, Greenland, Europe and Asia (excluding India) which began to break away from the single mass of *Pangea about 200 million years ago due to *sea-floor spreading.

Lava — Molten or semi-fluid magmatic rock that has erupted from a volcano or fissure in the Earth's surface. Also such rock that cooled and hardened. Though most of the lavas are *basic in composition they may range in composition from *acidic to *ultrabasic. Basaltic lavas often display *columnar jointing. A lava with an extremely rough spinose surface is called *Aa. A ropy looking lava is given the name *Pahoehoe.

Lava, Block — A lava whose surface is broken into large rectangular blocks.

Lava, Pillow — A basic lava that is composed of sack-like bodies packed together with finer-grained material in between, caused by sudden chilling in water.

Layered rocks — All rocks that display layered structures. Most sedimentary rocks are layered; some *lava flows are layered; igneous rocks which show banding that resemble stratification are layered; some metamorphic rocks also show crude layering due to arrangement of platy minerals..

Lebensspur (Pl. **Lebensspuren**) — A general term for a sedimentary structure made by biological activity including a *trace fossil and track or burrow made by living animals on newly-laid sediments.

Lectotype — A specimen of a fossil chosen as the type of a species or sub-species if the author of the name fails to designate a type.

Lens — A lens-shape body of rock of a different lithology than the unit that encloses it.

Lepidolite — A lithium mica, grey or liliac in colour; monoclinic; hardness about 3; sp. gr. 2.85.

Leucite — A potassium-aluminium feldspathoid, $KAlSi_2O_6$; cubic; hardness 6; sp. gr. 2.45–2.50; white, colourless.

Leucocratic — Light-coloured igneous rock containing less than 35% dark minerals.

Level — (1) A horizontal passage in a mine intended for regular working and transportation. (2) An approximately horizontal line or surface taken as an index of altitude.

Lias (Liassic) — Lower part of the *Jurassic, corresponding roughly with the standard Lower Jurassic, above the *Triassic and below *Dogger. It ranges from 208.0 to 178.0 Ma (GTS). According ot ICS-2004, the Lower Jurassic extended from 199.6 $\pm$ 06 to 175.6 $\pm$ 2.0 Ma.

Lignite — A usually brownish black *coal intermediate between *peat and *bituminous coal, particularly in which the texture of the original wood is distinct. Also called **Brown coal.**

Limburgite — A basic igneous rock consisting of *phenocrysts of *augite and *olivine embedded in a matrix of brown basaltic glass that occurs as *flows and *dykes.

Limestone — A sedimentary rock composed mainly of calcium carbonate ($CaCO_3$).

Limnology — Scientific study of lakes in all aspects, including their sediments.

Limonite — A brownish or yellowish massive, amorphous to cryptocrystalline iron ore which is a hydrous mixture of ferric oxides with variable composition.

Lineament — A large-scale linear topographical feature on the Earth's surface that is controlled structurally.

Lineation — The subparallel orientation of a variety of linear features in a rock. It may be orientation of minerals or rock particles.

Lithic — Relating to, like, or of, rocks.

Lithify — To transform into rock.

Lithofacies — (1) A term loosely applied to any particular kind of sedimentary rock. (2) A lateral, mappable subdivision of a particular stratigraphic unit, distinguished on the basis of lithological characters from adjacent sub-divisions.

Lithology — The physical characters of rocks.

Lithosome — A rock body of essentially uniform, or uniformly heterogeneous, lithologic character, having intertonguing relationship in all directions with adjacent bodies of different lithologic characters.

Lithosphre — The rigid part of the Earth's *crust, lying above the *asthenosphere, extending to a depth of about 65 km below the surface, and comprising the *sial the *sima and the upper *mantle.

Lithostratigraphic Unit — A body of rocks that is defined and recognized on the basis of its lithologic properties or combination of lithologic properties and stratigraphic relations. A lithostratigraphic unit may consist of sedimentary, or igneous, or metamorphic rocks. The name of a lithostratigraphic unit has two components: the first a geographical name and the other the rank or lithologic name, both words capitalized. The conventional hierarchy of formal lithostratigraphic terms are: **Supergroup**, **Group**, **Formation**, **Member**, **Bed**, **Flow.**

Lithostratigraphy — The element of *stratigraphy that deals with the description and nomenclature of the rocks of the Earth based on their *lithology and their stratigraphic relations.

Lit-par-lit injection — A structure of a layered rock whose laminae have been penetrated along the schistocity planes by numerous thin, roughly parallel sheets of igneous material, usually granite.

Littoral zone — The seaward coastal region between the high and low water marks.

Llandovery — The oldest series / epoch of the four-fold *Silurian, it extends from about 443.7 to about 428.2 Ma, overlying the *Ordovician and lying under the *Wenlock. It consists of three stages.

Load cast — A sole structure consisting of a swelling or somewhat irregular bulbous or mamillary feature on the base of a sandstone bed that extends downward into soft and finer-grained shaly sediment. It cannot be used to distinguish current direction.

Loam — A soil containing a mixture of varying proportions of clay, silt and sand.

Lode — A vein of metal *ore intruded into a joint or fissure or a system of joints or fissures in rocks.

Loess — A loosely compacted deposit or soil that is formed by deposition of *silt, generally calcareous, by wind action that occurs as a thick blanket on the surface.

Longitude — The angular distance of a place east or west of the standard Greenwich *prime meridian which is zero (0°). There are 180 longitudes east and 180 longitudes west of the prime meridian, each called a degree. The 180° coincidental meridian is also known as the **International Date Line.**

Lopingian — The top series / epoch of the three-fold *Permian, extending from about 260.4 to about 251.0 Ma, lying above the *Guadalupian and beneath the *Triassic. It consists of two stages.

Lopolith — A saucer-shaped mass of igneous rock caused by intrusion of magma into the *Lithosphere without reaching the surface, and differing from a **Sill** in that its upper surface forms a shallow basin.

Lower — The qualifier is applied to the name of a *chronostratigraphic unit (*System, *Series, *Stage) to indicate position in the geologic column and corresponds to *Early as applied to the name of an equivalent geologic-time unit (*Period, *Epoch, *Age).

Ludlow — A series / epoch of the four-fold *Silurian, lying above the *Wenlock and below the *Pridoli, and extending from about 422.9 to about 418.7 Ma. It consists of two stages.

Luminescence — Emission of light by a substance that has not been heated, as in **Fluorescence** and **Phosphorescence.**

Lustre — The appearance of the light reflected from the surface of a mineral.

Lustre, Adamantine — A lustre shown by sparkling, brilliant, transparent minerals with high refractive indices like that of a cut and polished diamond.

Lustre, Dull — A lustre shown by minerals or rocks with rough, porous surfaces, or fine-grained aggregates of minerals that diffuse light rather than reflect light; it is earthy in appearance.

Lustre, Glassy — Lustre displayed by minerals shining like glass, somewhat different from vitreous.

Lustre, Greasy — Minerals that have the appearance of resin show this type of lustre.

Lustre, Metallic — A lustre that is associated with opaque minerals that look like a metal.

Lustre, Pearly — A lustre given by transparent minerals shining like mother-of-pearl. *Syn.* Nacreous lustre.

Lustre, Silky — A shining lustre displayed by aggregates of thin, transparent and fibrous minerals.

Lustre, Splendant — A lustre displayed by minerals that cause reflection with brilliancy, giving well-defined images.

Lustre, Submetallic — Duller, metallic lustre of dark-coloured minerals with high refractive indices and of some opaque minerals reflecting part of the light.

Lustre, Vitreous — Lustre shown by transparent minerals shining like glazed china.

Lutites — Sedimentary rocks composed of very fine clay particles, like *mudstones, *siltstones and *shales. Another term is **Pelite**.

M

Maceral — One of the organic constituents of the coal mass. Macerals are to coal as minerals are to inorganic rock. Common macerals are *vitrain, *clarain, *durain, and * fusain.

Macrocrystalline — A rock or aggregate in which crystals are large enough to be visible to the naked eye.

Mafic — Relating to or denoting a group of dark-coloured, mainly *ferromagnesian minerals. such as *pyroxene and *olivine.

Magma — The molten material that exists below the solid rocks of the Earth's crust from which *lava and other *igneous rocks are formed by cooling.

Magnesite — A white carbonate mineral, composition $MgCO_3$; trigonal; massive, granular, compact; hardness 4; sp. gr. 3.

Magnetic declination — The horizontal angle at any given location between the *true north and the *magnetic north.

Magnetic dip / inclination — The direction of the Earth's magnetic field in terms of angle at which the field is inclined to the horizontal.

Magnetic north — The direction towards which the needle of a magnetic compass points. It differs from the *true north by a few degrees and/or minutes to the east or west of it for any given locality.

Magnetic pole — Either of the two small areas which are located respectively in the polar regions of the Northern and the Southern Hemispheres towards which a compass needle points from any direction on the Earth's surface. The two magnetic poles keep on shifting slightly over time.

Magnetite — A black iron oxide mineral, Fe_3O_4; cubic; hardness 6; sp. gr. 5.2; has very strong magnetism.

Magnetostratigraphy — The element of stratigraphy that deals with the magnetic characteristics of rock bodies.

Magnitude of Earthquake — *See* **Richter Scale.**

Malachite — A bright green carbonate mineral of copper, $Cu_2CO_3(OH)_2$; monoclinic; massive/encrustations; hardness 3.5 – 4; sp. gr.4.

Malleable — A metal or alloy capable of being hammered out of shape without returning to the original.

Malm — Upper part of the *Jurassic, corresponding roughly with the standard Upper Jurassic, lying above the *Doggar and below the *Cretaceous. It ranges from 157.1 to 145.6 Ma (GTS). According to ICS-2004, the upper Jurassic extends from 161.2 $\pm$ 4.0 to 145.5 $\pm$ 4.0 Ma.

Mammalia/Mammals — A large class of warm-blooded higher vertebrates that nourish their young with milk secreted by mamillary glands, and includes humans. They range from the *Jurassic to the present.

Mammoth — Extinct *Pleistocene mammal, distinguished from modern elephants by highly ridged molars, curved tusks, hairy body, belonging to genus *Mammonuthus*.

Mantle — The layer of rock below the Earth's crust, or the *lithosphere, and lying above the *core, consisting of rocks of higher density than those of the lithosphere, and separated from it by the **Moho**; it extends downwards to about 2900 km below the Earth's surface.

Marble — A recrystallised metamorphosed limestone and/or dolomite with *saccharoidal texture formed by thermal or regional metamorphism.

Marine geology — The aspect of geology involved in the study of the oceans that deals specifically with the ocean floor and the ocean-continental border, including the submarine relief features.

Marker bed — A bed that can be identified or correlated readily with respect to any specified character such as by *lithology, *paleontology or any other character.

Marl —.An unconsolidated sedimentary rock or soil consisting of clay and lime.

Mass wasting — A general term for the processes leading to breakdown and downslope movement of soil and rock material due to gravity.

Massif — A mountain mass that breaks up into peaks towards the summit, and has relatively uniform characteristics.

Mastodon — A large extinct mammal of the *Miocene to *Pleistocene age that differ from the related mammals and existing elephants chiefly in the form of the molar teeth.

Matrix — (1) The finer-grained material filling the interstices between larger grains or particles of a sediment or sedimentary rock (2) The *groundmass in an igneous rock.

Medial moraine — *See* **Moraine**.

Medical geology — The branch of geology involving studies of toxic and other elements in minerals, metals and rocks in relation to medical and health problems of humans and other animals.

Megacryst — A crystal in an igneous rock that is much larger than those surrounding it in the *groundmass.

Melange — A sedimentary deposit consisting of a jumbled mass of a wide range of various types and varieties of rock fragments and blocks of all sizes.

Melanocratic — A dark-coloured igneous rock containg more than 65% dark minerals. *Cf.* **Ultrabasic**; **Ultramafic**.

Member — The formal lithostratigraphic unit next in rank below a *formation. It possesses lithologic properties distinguishing it from adjacent parts of the formation.

Mesa — A high, flat, rocky, table-like isolated upland with precipitous slopes all around.

Mesocratic — A medium-coloured igneous rock containing 35–65 % dark minerals.

Mesostasis — *Groundmass in an igneous rock.

Mesothermal deposit — An *epigenetic mineral deposit, intermediate between *epithermal and *hypothermal deposit, formed at considerable depth and in the temperature range of 200°– 300°C.

Mesoproterozoic — The middle *geochronometric division of the three-fold *Proterozoic, base at 1600 Ma (above the *Statherian) and top at 1000 Ma (below the *Tonian); it is divided into the *Calymmian, *Ectasian, and *Stenian.

Mesozoic — The middle division (erathem/era) of the *Phanerozoic, extending from about 251 Ma to about 65.5 Ma ago, sub-divided into * Triassic, *Jurassic and *Cretaceous systems / periods. It was the age of giant reptiles and the beginning of mammalian life. There were extensive lava flows in India, South Africa and South America.

Metacrysts — *Syn.* of **Porphyroblast.**

Metal — A solid material which is typically hard, shiny, malleable, fusible and ductile with good electrical and thermal conductivity, and exception being mercury which is liquid.

Metallogenetic province — Said of a region in which a series of mineral deposits possess common characteristics.

Metallurgy — The branch of science and technology concerned with the properties, production and purification of metals.

Metamorphic aureole — The rock immediately surrounding a mass of intrusive igneous rock mass that has undergone metamorphism, mainly thermal, or changes by contact with it.

Metamorphic facies — A set of metamorphic mineral assemblage or rocks that have formed over the same range of physical conditions, and where differences in mineralogy are due to the variation in chemical composition of the original rock types.

Metamorphic grade — The degree of metamorphism considered by the amount of differentiation between the original parent rock and the later developed metamorphic rock.

Metamorphism — A pronounced change in the constitution of a rock effected by pressure, heat and water that results in a more compact and more highly crystalline condition.

Metamorphism, Contact — Thermal metamorphism induced by contact with igneous intrusions.

Metamorphism, Dynamic — Changes in rocks caused by intense localized stress that tend to break up the rocks, sometimes into fine powder.

Metamorphism, Regional — Change in rocks caused by large-scale action of both heat and pressure which produce a wide range of new minerals and a widespread development of structural changes. *Syn.* Dynamothermal metamorphism.

Metamorphism, Retrograde — *See* **Diaphthoresis**

Metamorphism, Thermal — Changes that occur in a rock in which only heat plays a part without significant pressure coming into play.

Metaquartzite — *See* **Quartzite**.

Metasomatism — A metamorphic process that occurs in a rock involving mineralogical and chemical changes due to interaction with migrating fluids introduced from an external source.

Metazoa — A major division of the animal kingdom, comprising all animals other than *Protozoa and *sponges that have bodies composed of cells differentiated into tissues and organs and usually a digestive cavity lined with special cells.

Meteorite — A piece of rock or metal that has fallen to the Earth as a meteor without completely disintegrating in the atmosphere. They are classified into siderites, siderolites, aerolites (stony meteorite) , tektites, and chondrites.

Methane — A colourless and odourless inflammable gas fuel which is the main constituent of natural gas hydrocarbon CH_4; it is a product of decomposition of organic matter and of the carbonization of *coal.

Micas — A group of common rock-forming minerals characterized by a layered structure which gives the crystals a platy form and a perfect basal cleavage where the cleavage flakes are flexible and elastic. They are chemically complex hydrous sheet silicates, commonly containing aluminium, potassium, sodium, magnesium and iron. Important members of the group are *muscovite, *biotite, *phlogopite, and *lepidolite.

Micrite — Microcrystalline calcite mud now forming the body of chemically precipitated calcareous rocks.

Microcline — A mineral of the feldspar group, $KAlSi_3O_8$; triclinic; prismatic; twinning common; hardness 6; sp. gr. 2.56. Part of the alkali or potash / potassium feldspar group.

Microcrystalline — A rock formed of microscopic crystals.

Microfossil — A fossil that can only be seen under the microscope.

Microlite — A very small crystal that can be recognized only under the microscope, usually found embedded in glassy material.

Microlith — A tiny blade tool of flint.

Micropalaeontology — A branch of *palaeontology that is concerned with the study of fossils too small to be observed without the aid of a microscope.

Microplate — A small tectonic *plate with identifiable margins.

Middle — The qualifier is applied to the name of a **chronostratigraphic unit** (*System, *Series, *Stage) to indicate position in the geologic column, and corresponds to *Middle as applied to the name of the equivalent geologic time unit (*Period, *Epoch, *Age).

Mid-Oceanic Ridges — *See* **Oceanic Ridges.**

Migmatite — A coarse heterogeneous gneissose rock consisting of bands and patches of quartz-feldspar granitic material and *mafic minerals consisting chiefly of *biotite or *hornblende.

Miller index — An index used in *crystallography to specify the orientation of a *crystal face.

Mine — A pit or excavation in the Earth from which mineral substances are taken out; it may be underground or open on the surface. *Cf.*, **Quarry.**

Mineral — The conventional definition is that it is a solid inorganic crystalline substance of natural occurrence. However, in the broadest sense it includes such products like *coal, *petroleum, natural gas, and even water, that are obtained from the bowls of the Earth.

Mineral, Economic — A mineral that can be utilized profitably by itself, of by a metal or other product extracted from it.

Mineral, Industrial — A mineral, rock or any other naturally occurring substance of economic value, generally nonmetallic, but excluding metallic ores, mineral fuels and gemstones.

Mineral, Rock-forming — Such a mineral that enters into the composition of rocks and determines its classification.

Mineral belt — An elongated region of liberalization containing several mineral deposits.

Mineral deposit — A naturally occurring body of a mineral that is wholly or partly of economic value.

Mineral fuels — A term to cover various types of *coals and *hydrocarbons.

Mineralography — The microscopic study of polished surface of opaque minerals, generally ore minerals, under reflected light.

Mineralogy — The scientific study of *minerals in all their aspects, including properties, classification, crystal structure and the ways to distinguish them.

Miocene — According to ICS-2004, the oldest series/epoch of the four-fold *Neogene, lasting from 23.03 to 6.332 Ma ago, lying above the *Oligocene and below the *Pliocene. Earlier, it was considered by ICS-2000 as the older of the two-fold *Neogene. It was the fourth series / epoch from the base of the traditional *Tertiary, a stratigraphic unit that is not recognised by IUGS. The Miocene was characterized by great mountain building episodes that formed the Himalayas and the Alps, and lead to the development of most modern mammalian groups; bony fishes became common and grasses were widespread.

Microcline — A generally pink *feldspar, composition $KAlSi_3O_8$; triclinic; twinning common; hardness 6; sp. gr. 2.56; bright green variety amazonite is used as an ornamental stone.

Miogeosyncline — A *geosyncline that has a thinner development of sediments than an *eugeosyncline and no volcanic rocks, forming adjacent to the *craton.

Mississippian — A North American system/period, but otherwise regarded by the Standard Global Chronostratigraphic Scale as the lower of subsystem / subperiod of the *Carboniferous, lying above the *Devonian and below the *Pennsylvanian, lasting between 360 and 320 Ma ago. The earliest winged insects appeared during this time.

Mobile belt — *Syn.* **Orogenic belt.**

Mode — The actual percentage by weight of the individual minerals which make up an igneous rock.

Modified Mercalli Scale — *See* **Intensity of Earthquake.**

Moho. / Mohorovicic Discontinuity — The seismic boundary or surface between the Earth's *Crust and the *Mantle; its average depth is 35 km, 5–10 km beneath the oceans, and 40–70 km beneath the continents.

Mohs' scale — A scale of hardness that is determined by the comparative resistance by which a mineral is scratched by another. It is checked with reference to a set of standard minerals, which consist of — from the softest to the hardest — 1. *Talc; 2. *Gypsum; 3. *Calcite; 4. *Fluorite; 5. *Apatite, 6. *Orthoclase; 7. *Quartz; 8. *Topaz; 9. *Corundum; 10. *Diamond. This is an empirical scale and the steps between two minerals are not of equal value.

Molasse — Commonly non-marine and partly deltaic sedimentary *facies consisting of very thick sequence of rocks like *arkoses, *conglomerates, *breccias, *marls and *shales produced by the erosion of mountain ranges after the final phases of *orogeny.

Mollusca / Mollusks — A large phylum of invertebrate animals with a soft unsegmented body, usually encased in a calcareous shell. It is divided into a number of important classes; *Amphineura, *Scaphopoda, *Gastropoda, *Lamellibranchiata (Pelecypoda, Bivalvia), *Cephalopoda (Nautilioidea, Ammonoidea, Belemnoidea).

Molybdenite — A blue-grey mineral of molybdenum, composition MoS_2; hardness 1; sp. gr. 4.7.

Monandnock — A remnant, isolated hill or mass of resistant rock which has been left standing above the surrounding peneplained country. It is similar to an **Inselberg.**

Monazite — A brown mineral consisting of a phosphate of rare earth elements and thorium occurring as an accessory mineral in acid igneous rocks. It is harvested from some sands as a *detrital mineral.

Monocline — A step-like flexture of stratified rock causing a local steepening of the *dip in otherwise horizontal or gently dipping beds.

Monoclinic system — A crystal system which has either a single two-fold axis of symmetry, a single plane of symmetry, or a combination of the two. Of the three axes, two, vertical and horizontal, are at right angles, with the third making an angle (other than a right angle) with the vertical axis, the plane defined by the vertical axis and the inclined axis being perpendicular to the horizontal axis. The three parameters are all unequal. It has three classes of symmetry.

Monomict — *Syn.* **Oligomict.**

Montmorillonite — A hydrous aluminium-rich clay mineral group which has considerable capacity for exchanging a part of the aluminium for magnesium and bases on absorbing water. Also called **Fuller's earth** group.

Monzonite — Coarse-grained saturated igneous rocks ranging from acid *quartz-bearing type to basic *olivine-bearing varieties containing approximately equal amounts of alkali *feldspar and *plagioclase; it is intermediate between *syenite and *diorite. *Syn.* **Syenodioriote.**

Moraine — It is a poorly sorted and often angular rock detritus transported by glaciers and ice sheets. It is of several types.

Moraine, Englacial — Material which has fallen into the glacier and is carried down the valley embedded in ice.

Moraine, Ground — It is formed as a sheet of material, usually tens of metres thick, with a surface characterized by very low relief.

Moraine, Lateral — A ridge of material along the side of a valley formerly occupied by a glacier.

Moraine, Medial — A ridge or spread of material extending lengthwise along the center of a glacier; it may be caused by meeting of two glaciers.

Moraine, Subglacial — Material near the base of ice which has either sunk through the ice has been torn up from the valley floor by ice.

Moraine, Terminal — An accumulation of material that develops against the front of a glacier due to melting of ice.

MSK (Medvedev-Sponheuer-Karnik) Scale — *See* **Intensity of Earthquake.**

Mud cracks — Irregular polygonal cracks that develop in rocks, originally a mud, as a result of shrinkage on drying. Some cracks get filled later with extraneous material. Some cracks may be seen on the rock surface, but some cracks may be preserved on the underside of the overlying sandstone bed as a polygonal network of elevated sharp-crested ridges. *Syn.* ***Desication cracks,** Sun cracks.

Mudstone — A dark sedimentary rock formed from consolidated mud and lacking the *lamination of *shale.

Mud volcano — A small cone-like structure in poorly consolidated lands and clays through which mud and gases are erupted.

Multiple twinning — *See* **Twinning, Polysynthetic.**

Muscovite — A colourless **member** of the potassium *mica group; monoclinic; platy; hardness 2.5–3; sp. gr. 2.76–3.

Mylonite — A highly granular and sheared metamorphic rock without cleavage but banded or streaky, in which the individual crystals are fractured or crushed; it is produced by intense dynamic metamorphism or tectonic dislocation.

N

Nacre — The hard, iridescent internal layer of pearl consisting chiefly of calcium carbonate (principally *aragonite) deposited in layers and interleaved with thin sheets of organic matrix.

Nanofossil — Extremely small marine fossils, primarily calcareous, smaller than *microfossils.

Nappe — A huge recumbent fold with both the limbs practically horizontal which has been forced a great distance, of possibly several kilometres, over the underlying formations thus covering them.

Natural gas — Combustible gas, consisting mainly of methane and other **Hydrocarbons**, occurring naturally underground in the Earth's crust and used as a fuel.

Nautiloidea/Nautiloids — A sub-class of *Cephalopoda, they are characterized by a centrally located siphuncle and by a straight, curved or coiled chambered external shell with less elaborate suture flextures than in ammonites. They range from the Upper *Cambrian to the present though they were abundant in the *Ordovician and especially in the*Silurian; they are represented in today's fauna only by the genus *Nautilus*.

Neck — Same as **Plug.**

Nematoblastic — A *homoblastic type of metamorphic texture of *schists in which *foliation is produced by development during recrystallisation of parallel prismatic minerals, such as *hornblende and *augite.

Neoblast — A crystal that is often formed later than the other grains of the same or other mineral species in a metamorphic rock.

Neogene — According to ICS-2004 the upper system / period of the two-fold *Cenozoic, starting at 23.03 ago and continuing to the present. The Neogene now has four series / epochs, viz., *Miocene, *Pliocene, *Pleistocene, and *Holocene. Earlier, the Neogene according to ICS-2000 was divided into two series / epochs of *Miocene and *Pliocene; it started at 23.5 Ma ago at the base of the *Miocene and lasted till 1.7 Ma ago at the top of the *Pliocene at the boundary with the *Pleistocene , which was considered the lower division of the *Quaternary system/period of the earlier two-fold Neogene. During this time the African rifts appeared, and there was a prolonged period of mountain building in South America.

Neoproterozoic — The upper *geochronometric division of the three-fold *Proterozoic ranging from 1000 Ma (above the *Stenian) to 542 Ma (below the *Cambrian); it is sub-divided into *Tonian, *Cryogenian, and *Ediacaran.

Neotectonics — The tectonic movements or activities of the Earth's crust during the *Neogene and later times.

Neotype — A *type specimen of a fossil that is selected subsequent to the description of a species to replace a pre-existing type that has been lost or destroyed.

Nephelene — A colourless to greenish *feldspathoid, composition $(Na,K)AlSiO_4$; hexagonal; irregular massive; hardness 6; sp. gr. 2.6.

Nephrite — A variety of *tremolite-actinolite, green or white, a less valuable kind of jade.

Neritic — Pertaining to the shallow water environment lying between the low tide level and a depth of about 200 metres on the continental shelf. *Syn.* **Sublittoral.**

Névé — Uncompacted granular snow, especially at the head of a glacier. *Syn.* **Firn.**

Nicol prism — A prism for producing plane polarized light consisting of two pieces of optically clear *calcite, cemented together with *Canada balsam.

Nodule — A rounded lump of mineral or mineral aggregate, not more than 256 mm in diameter, usually of contrasting composition from the enclosing sediment.

Nonconformity — This type of break occurs when sedimentary rocks lie over the older plutonic igneous or massive metamorphic rocks that were exposed to erosion before they were covered by the overlying strata.

Norm — *See* **CIPW normative classification.**

Normal fault — A fault with a dominant dip-slip component in which the *hanging wall is on the *downthrow side relative to the footwall.

Nuée ardente — An incandescent cloud of gas, ash and lava fragments ejected out from a volcano, typically as a part of a *pyroclastic flow.

Nugget — A small lump of gold (or other *precious metals) generally found in alluvial deposits.

Nummulite — The fossilized disc-shaped calcareous shell of a family belonging to the *foraminifer order.

Nunatak — An isolated peak or hill projecting above a surface of inland snow and ice sheet (as in Antarctica and Greenland).

O

Oblate — A spheroid flattened at the poles (said of a rock particle). *Cf.* **Prolate.**

Obsidian — A hard, dark, glass-like volcanic rock formed by the rapid solidification of lava without crystallization.

Oceanic ridges — Very large undersea mountain ranges, rising 1–4 km above the surrounding sea floor that wind their way around the globe for over 80,000 km and cover 35% of the sea floor; average depth of a ridge crest is about 2.5 km, and the ridge width is 2000–4000 km. Also called **Mid-Oceanic Ridges**.

Oceanic trench — A long, narrow depression in the sea floor, typically 50–100 km wide and up to several thousand km long, descending three to four km deeper than the surrounding sea floor.

Oceanography — The science dealing with the physical, chemical and biological properties and phenomena of the sea.

Ocellar — An igneous rock texture due to the presence of radiating groups of platy minerals with indistinct outlines.

Ochre — A red, brown or yellow earthy material containing ferric oxide.

Offlap — An unconformity that occurs when the lower beds of the upper series of rocks extend further than the younger ones. This is reverse of **overlap.**

Offshore — The zone situated some distance from the shore, extending from the lowest limit of low tide to the edge of the continental shelf.

Oil shale — A fine-grained, dark-coloured argillaceous rock containing *kerogens that yields liquid *hydrocarbons on distillation.

Oligocene — The youngest of the three series/epochs of the *Palaeogene, lasting from about 33.9 Ma ago to 23.03 Ma ago, lying above the *Eocene and below the *Miocene. Traditionally, it formed the third oldest series/epoch of the five-fold *Tertiary, an old stratigraphic unit not recognized now by ICS of IUGS. It was characterized by colder climate, general retreat of the seas, and movement of the Earth's crust to form the Himalayan and Alpine mountain chains. During this time many modern mammals developed, such as pachyderms, canines and felines, along with crabs, mussels and snails; forests diminished and grasses appeared.

Oligoclase — *See* **Plagioclase feldspars.**

Oligomict — Said of a *clastic sedimentary rock composed of a single rock type. *Syn.* **Monomict.**

Olivines — A group of rock-forming silicates, $(Mg,Fe)_2SiO_4$; orthorhombic; granular massive; hardness 6.5; about 3.4; green in colour.

Oncolite — A small, variously shaped, concentrically laminated, calcareous concretionary structure formed by accretion of layers of gelatinous sheaths of blue-green algae that superficially resembles concretions.

Onlap — *Syn.* of **Overlap.**

Oolite — An allochemical limestone formed essentially from **ooliths.**

Oolith — Nearly spherical, very small (about up to 2 mm diameter) bodies formed by the precipitation of *carbonates in concentric layers around a nucleus.

Ooze — Wet mud or slime, especially that found at the bottom of a body of water.

Opal — A hydrated amorphous silica mineral used as a semi-precious stone, typically semi-transparent and often marked by iridescent play of colours.

Opalescence — A phenomenon of light showing marked play of iridescent colours.

Opaque mineral — A mineral that does not transmit light and appears black in a thin section in plane polarized light under the microscope.

Opencast — (1) A method of mining in which *coal or *ore is extracted at or from a level near the Earth's surface, rather than from *shafts. (2) Such a *mine.

Ophiolite — An assemblage of *ultramafic and *mafi intrusive an extrusive rocks widely believed to occur in oceanic crust, consisting largely of serpentine.

Ophitic — A holocrystalline, *hypidiomorphic granular texture characteristic of some basic igneous rocks consisting of large *pyroxene or *hornblende crystals enclosing, partially or wholly, laths of *plagioclase.

Ordovician — The second oldest geological system/period of the *Paleozoic between the *Cambrian and the *Silurian, extending from about 488.3 to about 443.7 Ma ago. It consists of three series / epochs. There was much volcanic activity and marine sedimentation. Numerous invertebrates flourished, including *graptolites, *trilobites, *brachiopods and *corals; and the first vertebrates (jawless fish) appeared.

Ore — A mineral deposit from which metallic and non-metallic constituents can be extracted profitably.

Ore dressing — Mechanical preparation, as by crushing, and concentration of ore, as by floatation, to make it ready for processing or smelting.

Organic deposits — A sedimentary deposit that consists of the remains of organisms (plants or animals) or is derived from organic matter, such as coal or oil.

Orocline — An orogenic belt that has a marked change in trend resulting from folding and faulting by horizontal forces operating within the crust.

Orogenic belt — A long linear area of the Earth's crust which had undergone intense deformation, often accompanied by seismic and volcanic activity. *Syn.* **Mobile belt.**

Orogeny/Orogenesis — Mountain building that is caused by change in the level of the Earth's crust in which rocks are thrown up into folds or blocks to form ranges and mountains.

Orography — The branch of physical geology and geography that deals with surface relief, particularly in respect of mountains.

Orosirian — A *geochronometric sub-division of the four-fold *Paleoproterozoic, dated between 2050 and 1800 Ma ago, placed above the *Rhyacian and below the *Statherian.

Orpiment — An orange-coloured vitreous mineral of arsenic, As_2S_3; monoclinic; hardness 2; sp. gr. 3.48.

Orthoclase — A mineral of the feldspar group, $KAlSi_3O_8$; monoclinic; prismatic; twinning common; hardness 6; sp.gr. 2.56; white to pink in colour; part of the alkali or potash / potassium feldspar group.

Orthoquartzite — *See* **Quartzite**.

Orthorhombic system — A crystal system in which the three axes are mutually at right angles, all of different lengths; it has three classes of symmetry.

Ostrocoda / Ostrocods — A class of mostly fresh-water, very small-sized *arthropods that have the body enclosed in a bivalve *carapace, the body segments obscured, the abdomen rudimentary and only seven pairs of appendages. They range from the *Cambrian to the present.

Outcrop — That part of a rock formation which is visible on the surface of the Earth.

Outlier — An exposed area of younger rock formations completely surrounded by older rocks, usually due to erosion, faulting or folding. It is opposite of **Inlier.**

Overburden — Any barren, loose or rock material overlying a mineral deposit that must be removed before mining.

Overgrowth — A deposit of secondary mineral in optical and crystallographic continuity around a crystal grain of the same composition. Also *see* **Authigenesis**.

Overlap — An unconformity that occurs when progressively younger members of the upper rock series rest upon the older rock series.

Overthrust — A low-angle *thrust fault of large scale, with displacement generally measured in kilometers.

P

Pahoehoe — *Lava having a ropy or corded surface.

Palaeoblast (Paleoblast) — A crystal, or remnant of a crystal, that is older than the other grains of the same or other mineral species in a metamorphic rock.

Palaeobotany (Paleobotany) — A branch of botany concerned with the study of fossil plants, a part of the overall science of **Palaeontology.**

Palaeocene (Paleocene) — The early series / epoch of the three fold *Palaeogene, lasting from about 65.5 Ma ago, lying at the top of the *Cretaceous, extending to the boundary with the *Eocene at about 55.8 Ma ago. Traditionally, it formed the oldest epoch / series of the five-fold Tertiary, a stratigraphic unit not recognized by ICS of IUGS. During this time, there was widespread subsidence of land and considerable volcanic activity. The vast majority of dinosaurs became extinct and mammals suddenly diversified with the appearance of the first primates; flowering plants were widespread.

Palaeoclimate (Paleoclimate) — A climate prevalent at a particular time in the geological past.

Palaeoecology (Paleoecology) — The ecology (the inter-relationship of organisms and their environment) of fossil animals and plants.

Palaeocurrent (Paleocurrent) — An ancient current of water that existed in the geological past, whose direction is inferred from the *sedimentary structures and *textures of the rocks formed at that time.

Palaeogene (Paleogene) — The earlier system/period of the two-fold *Cenozoic according to the new ICS-2004, extending from the base at about 65.5 Ma ago to 23.03 Ma ago at the top at the boundary with *Miocene. Earlier, ICS-2000 had placed it as the oldest division of the three-fold Cenozoic. Traditionally, it formed a part of the oldest five-fold classical *Tertiary, an old stratigraphic unit that is not recognized by ICS of IUGS. During this time, the continents took the present form. It was the early age of mammals; many modern types of animals and plants appeared.

Palaeogeography (Paleogeography) — The study of geographical features at the times or periods in the geological past.

Palaeolimnology (Paleolimnology) — The study of lake sediments to interpret lake conditions.

Palaeomagnetism (Paleomagnetism) — Branch of geophysics concerned with the magnetism preserved in rocks which contain iron-bearing minerals that was induced by the Earth's magnetic field at the time of their formation.

Palaeontology (Paleontology) — The branch of science concerned with *fossil animals and plants. In popular parlance it is used for the study of fossil animals only, the branch concerned with plants is referred to as **Palaeobotany.**

Palaeoproterozoic (Paleoproterozoic) — The lower *geochronometric division of the three-fold *Proterozoic ranging from 2500 Ma (above the *Archaean) to 1600 Ma (below the *Calymmian); it is sub-divided into *Siderian, *Rhyacian, *Orosirian, and *Statherian.

Palaeosol (Paleosol) — A stratum or soil horizon which was formed as a soil in a past geological age.

Palaeozoic (Paleozoic) — The oldest of the three erathems/eras of the *Phanerozoic extending from 542.0 to 251.0 Ma ago. It is divided into six systems / periods, namely : *Cambrian (oldest), *Ordovician, *Silurian, *Devonian, *Carboniferous, and *Permian.

Palagonite — Hydrated basaltic glass, usually orange, yellow or brown, formed when basalts get erupted beneath water or ice.

Palingenesis — *Syn.* of **Anatexis**

Palynology — A branch of science concerned with the study of pollen grains and other spores, especially found in geological deposits.

Pangaea — The name given to the hypothetical supercontinent comprising *Gondwanaland and *Laurasia which made up the Earth's single continental crust before the *Jurassic Period. It began to split as a result of *continental drift, eventually forming the present-day distribution of continents.

Panidiomorphic — Relating to a texture formed by essentially *euhedral grains constituting an igneous rock.

Panthalassa — The ocean surrounding **Pangaea**

Paraconformity — An obscure or uncertain break or unconformity in which no erosional surface is discernable or in which the contact is a simple bedding plane and in which beds above and below the break are parallel as shown by surface of the same type of sedimentary rock. It is a break in continuity of deposition with faunal or other evidence of a time gap.

Paragenesis — A characteristic association or occurrence of minerals or mineral assemblages in ore deposits, indicating contemporaneous formation.

Parageosyncline — A *geosyncline lying within a *craton or stable area.

Paratype — Additional fossil specimen selected with a *holotype to show additional character of the species that are not shown by the holotype.

Particle — A term used in geology for a distinct, separable unit of a rock without regard to its shape, size, or composition.

Particle size, rudaceous rocks — The particle size classification of * rudaceous sedimentary rocks is given below. Rounded *clasts make up *conglomerates and angular clasts, *brecia.

2 – 4	mm	*Granule
4 – 64	mm	*Pebble
64 – 256	mm	*Cobble
> 256	mm	*Boulder

Parting lineation — A faint but distinct subparallel, structure consisting of linear grooves and ridge formed by grains of very slight relief on parting surfaces of bedding or splitting planes of some sandstones. They occur parallel to the direction of depositing currents, but the direction of current cannot be deduced as they are bi-directional. *Syn.* **Current lineation.**

Patina — A superficial layering of mineral matter on a rock surface, such as iron oxide coating on an exposed rock or boulder surface, often caused by capillary action.

Pay streak — A zone of concentrated *heavy minerals in a *placer deposit.

Peat — A partly decomposed carbonized vegetable matter forming a deposit on acidic, boggy ground. It is the first stage of *coal formation.

Pebble — (1) A small, usually smoothed and rounded stone, especially when worn out by the action of water. (2) As a size term it is a particle between*granule and *cobble, 4–64 mm in diameter.

Pediment — A gently sloping surface cut into bedrock where there is a change in gradient, such as at the foot of a steep hill slope, and extending towards an alluvial or river plain.

Pedology — The study of soil as a natural phenomenon, its chemistry, physics and microbiology, including its formation and development.

Pegmatite — (1) An exceptionally coarse-grained igneous rock of mainly granitic composition having a complex mineralogy, with *crystals larger than 3 cm, occasionally reaching a metre or so in length, sometimes larger; it usually occurs as *dykes, *lenses and *veins. (2) Also used as a textural term.

Pelagic — Relating to marine life zone in the water of the open sea, distinguished from **Benthic.**

Pelecypoda — *See* **Lamellibranchiata.**

Pele's hair — A mass of thread-like filaments of glass that is formed as a result of lava being exuded through a small opening and blown about by wind.

Pelites — *Syn.* of **Lutites.**

Pellet — A spherical or elliptical or ovoid particle of small size (0.25–5 mm) made up of *clay or *micrite, having no internal structure, believed to be excreted by some invertebrate animal.

Penecontemporaneous — Referring to geological events that appear to have occurred almost at the same time.

Peneplain — A region or land surface of considerable area of slight relief shaped by erosion.

Pennsylvanian — A North American system / period, but otherwise regarded in the Standard Global Chronostratigraphic Scale as a sub-system / sub-period, lying above the *Mississippian and below the *Permian, 320 to 290 Ma ago; approximately equivalent of Upper *Carboniferous. Contains much coal, and earliest reptile fossils.

Periclase — A colourless cubic mineral consisting of magnesium oxide, occurring chiefly in marble and limestone.

Pericline — (1) In structural geology, a general term for a fold in which the dip of the beds has a central orientation, beds dipping away from a center from a *dome, and beds dipping away towards a center to form a basin. (2) In mineralogy, a variety of albite (*plagioclase feldspar).

Peridot — A green semi-precious variety of forsterite, an orthorhombic mineral of *olivine group.

Peridotite — An ultrabasic *plutonic igneous rock consisting essentially of *olivine with or without minor *ferromagnesian minerals. It generally gets altered to *serpentine.

Periglacial — Relating to or denoting an area adjacent to a *glacier or *ice sheet or otherwise subjected to repeated freezing and thawing.

Period — *See* **System.**

Permafrost — A thick subsurface layer of soil on the Earth that remains below freezing point throughout the year.

Permeability — The property or capacity of a porous rock, sediment, or soil for transmitting a fluid.

Permian — The uppermost system/period of the *Palaeozoic extending from about 299 to about 251 Ma ago. It is divided into three series / epochs, namely, *Cisuralian, *Guadalupian and *Lopingian. It was marked by the extinction of many groups of marine invertebrates, the most important being the *trilobites, and some shell fishes, and the diversification and dominance of reptiles with development of many species of insects. Some mountains were formed, hot deserts existed in some pars of the

Earth, and there were periods of glaciation in the Southern Hemisphere.

Permo-Triassic — The *Permian and *Triassic considered as a single unit when the boundary between the two is often difficultt to delineate.

Perovskite — A black or brown mineral, composition $CaTiO_3$; cubic; hardness 5.5; sp. gr. 4.

Perthite — An intergrowth of potash feldspar and albite in which the albite occurs as patches or lenticles in the orthoclase host.

Petrification — The process of converting (organic matter) into rock. by infiltration of water and the deposition of dissolved mineral matter, as in fossilification.

Petrify — To convert (organic matter) into rock by encrusting or replacing its original substance with a mineral deposit, as in fossilization.

Petrochemical — (1) Relating to the chemical properties and processing of petroleum and natural gas. (2) Relating to the chemistry of rocks. (3) A chemical obtained from petroleum and natural gas.

Petrofabric — The complete spatial and geometrical configuration of all those components (texture, structure, orientation) that make up a deformed rock.

Petrofacies / Petrographic facies — A facies distinguished primarily on the basis of appearance or composition without taking into consideration the form, boundaries, or mutual relations.

Petrogenesis — The origin or mode of formation of rocks.

Petrography — A branch of geology dealing with the study of the composition and properties of rocks, both in hand specimen and under the microscope.

Petroleum — An oily flammable bituminous liquid, a complex mixture of *hydrocarbons and other substances, that occurs in some places in the upper strata of the Earth.

Petrological microscope — A special microscope for study of rock and mineral thin sections that uses polarized light and a rotating stage, with one *Nicol prism above and the other below the stage. *Syn.* **Polarising microscope.**

Petrology — A branch of geology that deals with all aspects of study of rocks : their description, systematic classification, origin, history, structure, composition, etc.

Phacolith — A lensoid intrusion of igneous rock occurring near the top of an anticline, with the concave surface facing downward.

Phaneritic / Phenocrystalline — Said of an igneous rock in which the constituent mineral grains can be seen with the naked eye.

Phanerozoic — The youngest of the eons / eonothems into which geologic time of rock bodies is divided. It starts from the end of the *Precambrian at about 542 Ma ago to the present time. It is divided into three eras/erathems, the oldest to the youngest, namely, the *Paleozoic, the *Mesozoic and the *Cenozoic (so named for the evidence of abundant life in its rocks).

Pheniclast — A large or conspicuous fragment in a sedimentary rock composed of various sizes of material, such as a *cobble or *pebble.

Phenoclast — (1) A large and conspicuous fragment in a sedimentary rock composed of various sizes of materials (such as *cobbles and *pebbles) embedded in a fine-grained matrix or groundmass. (2) individual components or fragments of a *conglomerate or *breccia.

Phenocryst — A relatively large, conspicuous, generally *euhedral crystal set in a fine-grained *matrix or *groundmass occurring in a porphyritic igneous rock.

Phenotype — The observable characteristic of an individual fossil resulting from the interaction of its *genotype with the environment. Also *See* **Genotype.**

Phlogopite — A usually brown to red magnesium mica; monoclinic; lamillar plates; hardness 2.5–3; sp. gr. 2.78–2.85.

Phonolite — A grey or green, fine-grained volcanic rock composed essentially of alkali *feldspars and *nepheline.

Phosphorescence — Light emitted by a substance without combustion or perceptible heat.

Phosphorite — A sedimentary rock rich in calcium phosphate.

Photogeology — A branch of geology concerned with the identification of geological features through the use of aerial or satellite photographs, such as geological mapping on photographs.

Photogrammetry — The technique of producing reliable measurements by using aerial photographs, particularly by using stereo pairs.

Phreatic water — *See* **Water, Phreatic.**

Phyllite — A layered siliceous metamorphic rock intermediate in texture and grain size between *slate and *schist, often showing silky sheen due to formation of mainly *sericite and subordinate *chlorite; it is formed by low temperature regional metamorphism.

Phylum (Pl. **Phyla**) — A principal taxonomic category of animals that ranks above the class and below a kingdom, equivalent to the division in botany.

Physical Geology — *Syn.* of **Dynamical geology.**

Physiography — The science that deals with the exterior physical features and changes of the Earth.

Picrite — An dark-coloured ultramafic rock consisting of *ferromagnesian minerals *olivine along with *pyroxene and *biotite, and accessory calic *plagioclase feldspar.

Piedmont — A gentle slope leading from the foot of a mountain to a region of comparatively flat land.

Pigeonite — A white to pale green monoclinic mineral of the pyroxene group which has general physical properties like those of *diopside.

Pillar — A solid mass of *coal, *rock, or *ore left standing to support a mine roof.

Pillow lava — A *lava having the appearance of pillows piled one upon another when it is chilled suddenly on contact with water.

Pilotaxitic — The texture of a glass-free volcanic rock, defined by felt-like masses of minute crystals.

Pinacoid — An open crystal form whose faces are parallel to two of the axes.

Pipe — A volcanic vent in the shape of a pipe intrusive through country rock.

Pisces (Fishes) — A numerous group of cold-blooded strictly aquatic vertebrate animals. The earliest fishes were jawless forms which later gave rise to the true jawed fishes. The earliest jawless fishes appeared in the *Silurian. They are found up to the present.

Pisolite — An allochemical limestone formed essentially from **pisoliths.**

Pisolith — Nearly spherical bodies formed by the precipitation of carbonate in concentric layers, more than 2 mm in diameter around a nucleus; they are larger than **Ooliths.**

Pitch (of fold) — *See* **Fold**.

Pitchblende — A massive form of the mineral *uraninite, contains radium, chief *ore of uranium.

Pithead — The top of a mining pit or *coal shaft.

Placer — A surfacial *alluvial, *eluvial, or *colluvial deposit which contains concentration of economically valuable *heavy minerals.

Plagioclase feldspars — A group of triclinic feldspar minerals of the series Albite-Oligoclase-Andesine-Labradorite-Bytonite-Anorthite; triclinie prismatic; hardness 6–6.5; sp. gr. 2.62–2.72; *Syn.* **Soda-lime; Sodium-calcium feldspars.**

Planetology — A science that applies the principles and techniques of geology and related sciences to the study of planetary bodies.

Plankton — The small and microscopic organisms drifting or floating in the sea or fresh water, consisting chiefly of *diatoms, *protozoans, small *crustaceans, and the eggs and larva stages of larger animals.

Plate — According to the theory of *plate tectonics, one of several large blocks or segments of rigid continental or oceanic material of which the Earth's crust or lithosphere is composed. A constructive plate is that which is situated at the *mid-oceanic ridge where new ocean floor is continuously being produced. A destructive plate is that which slides down beneath another plate.

Plate tectonics — The theory proposes that the Earth's *lithosphere is made up of a number of plates which may include both continental and oceanic *crust and which may move relative to one another. Plate boundaries are defined by major *earthquake zones and belts of volcanic activities. New plate material is generated by basaltic *lavas erupted along *mid-oceanic ridges and eventually is consumed at *subduction zones at the site of deep oceanic trenches. Plate collusions give rise to formation of mountain belts such as the Himalayas and the Alps. *The theory of *continental drift is explained by plate tectonics.

Playa — An area of flat-floored bottom of an undrained desert basin that at times becomes a shallow lake.

Pleistocene — According to ICS-2004, a series/epoch of the four-fold *Neogene, from 1.806 to 0.0115 Ma ago, lying above the *Pliocene and below the *Holocene. Earlier, ICS-2000 considered it as the older of the two series/epochs of the *Quaternary. It is also termed the *Ice Age in the Northern Hemisphere, where it is characterized by several periods of glacial advance and retreat causing seas to rise and fall. It was marked by the extinction of some mammals like the *mammoth and the *mastadon, and the evolution of man and familiar mammalian life; many plants perished.

Pleistogene — Term proposed as a replacement for the term **Quaternary** (GTS).

Pleochroism — The property of a crystal of showing different colours when viewed by light that vibrates parallel to different axes, especially viewed under a polarizing microscope.

Pliocene — According to ICS-2004, a series/epoch of the *Neogene, from 5.332 to 1.806 Ma, lying above the *Miocene and below the *Pleistocene. Earlier, it was considered by ICS-2000 as the younger of the two-fold Neogene. It was the youngest series/epoch of the traditional *Tertiary, a stratigraphic unit no longer recognized by ICS of IUGS. During this time, the continents and oceans adopted the present form, and giant sharks became extinct but many fish varieties developed; some plants and mammals died out but primates flourished.

Plug — (1) A roughly cylindrical, vertically-disposed body of intrusive rock, usually of small size. (2) A mass or column of solidified lava filling the central vent of a volcano. Also called a **Neck.**

Plunge (of fold) — *See* **Fold**.

Pluton — A typically large body of intrusive igneous rock.

Plutonic rocks — These are medium- to coarse-grained igneous rocks formed at great depths.

Pluvial — Relating to or characterized by rainfall.

Pneumatolysis — A process occurring during the final stages of crystallization of acid igneous rocks that brings about mineralogical changes in the crystalline parent rock, brought about by the action of hot gaseous substances (other than water).

Poikilitic — The texture found in some igneous rocks because of the presence of crystals enclosing inclusions of numerous smaller crystals of a different mineral.

Poikloblastic — A metamorphic rock texture in which large *metacrysts enclose inclusions of smaller crystals of a different mineral.

Polarization — The action or process of light so that the vibrations of the transverse wave is in one direction. This property is used to study minerals under crossed nicols in a *polarizing microscope.

Polarizer — A devise for polarizing light in a *petrological microscope, such as the lower *Nicol prism or the *Polaroid. Also *See* **Analyzer.**

Polarizing miroscope — *Syn.* **Petrological microscope.**

Polaroid — A trademark name for a sheet of cellulose that is impregnated with crystals of quinine idosulphate, so aligned that their optic axes are parallel and they polarize light in two directions at right angles. They replace *Nicol prisms in several types of *petrological microscopes.

Polar wandering — Long periods of the movement of the Earth's poles which may have occurred during the passage of geologic time.

Pollen — A mass of microspore in a seed plant appearing usually as a fine dust.

Polymict — Said of a clastic sedimentary rock composed of more than one mineral or rock type.

Polymorphism — (1) The occurrence of an element in two or more crystal forms possessing different atomic structures and therefore different properties. Example : Carbon crystallizing as *diamond in the *cubic system and *graphite in the *rhombohedral. (2) The existence of a species in several forms independent of sexual variations, especially referring to different types of individuals within a colony, as in *bryozoans or *corals.

Polyp — The sedentary form of a *coelentertate, typically columnar with the mouth uppermost and surrounded by a ring of tentacles.

Polysynthetic twinning — *See* **Twinning, Laminar.**

Polyzoa — *See* **Bryozoa.**

Porcellanite — A dense siliceous sedimentary rock having the texture, dull lustre, hardness, conchoidal fracture, and general appearance of unglazed porcelain occurring in alternating coloured layers or laminations.

Porifera/Porifers — A phylum of many-celled aquatic invertebrate animals characterized by an internal skeleton composed mostly of silica, and less commonly of calcium carbonate, that comprise the *sponges. They range from the *Precambrian to the present.

Porosity — The ratio or percentage of the bulk volume of a rock or soil that is occupied by interstices.

Porphyritic — Said of an igneous rock composed of grains / crystals of relatively large sizes, usually *euhedral, in a *groundmass or *marix of uniform grains.

Porphyroblast — A large crystals developed in a metamorphic rock by recrystallisation, such as a *garnet in *mica schist. *Syn.* **Metacryst**.

Porphyry — A hard igneous rock containing conspicuous *phenocrysts in a fine-grained *groundmass.

Potassic rock — In the IUGS classification, an igneous rock in which the molecular ratio $K_2O/Na_2O > 1$, or one in which weight percentage $K_2O > Na_2O$-2.

Potassium-argon (K-Ar) dating — Determination of the age of a mineral or rock in years, based on measurement of radiogenic argon-40 to potassium-40 and the known radioactive decay rate of potassium-40 to argon-40.

Pozzolan / Pozzolana — A finely ground siliceous material, such as diatomaceous earth, slag, tuff, etc., that is combined with Portland cement used for mortar.

Precambrian — The older of the two major divisions into which the geologic time and rocks have been conventionally divided according to modern stratigraphic usage, the other being the *Phanerozoic. It started with the informal style of 'pre-Cambrian' or 'Pre-Cambrian' and later got established as a formal unit of the Standard Global Chronostratigraphic Scale comprising all the rocks formed before the beginning of the *Cambrian at 542 Ma when the first abundant hard-bodied fossils appeared. It started from the time the Earth is believed to have come into existence about 4560 Ma ago and spans 88% of the Earth's history. The Precambrian time has been classified according to several different schemes. ICS no longer gives it a formal unit status, and it is defined in terms of *chronometric units of *Hadean, *Archaean, and *Proterozoic.

Precious metals — A group of metals that include gold, silver and platinum.

Precious stone — A highly attractive and valuable piece of mineral used especially in jewellery.

Precipice — A high, steep or vertical rock face of a *cliff or mountain.

Pridoli — The uppermost/youngest series/epoch of the four-fold *Silurian, about 148.7 to about 416.0 Ma, lying over the *Ludlow and beneath the *Devonian.

Primary mineral — A mineral formed at the same time as the rock enclosing it by igneous, hydrothermal or pneumatolysis processes, and that it retains its original composition and form. *Cf.* **Scondary mineral.**

Primate — An order of placental mammals that includes humans, apes, and related forms. First fossils found in the *Paleocene; continued into the present.

Prime meridian — The meridian of 0° longitude which runs through the original site of the Royal Observatory at Greenwhich, England, and from where other *longitudes are reckoned.

Priscoan — Chronometrically all the pre-Archaean time, encompassing the early history not only of the Solar System but of early cosmic events back to the beginning (e.g., to the 'Big Bang'). The term was adopted in *A Geologic Time Scale 1989* (GTS).

Prism — An open crystal form whose faces are parallel to one axis, especially the vertical axis, but meet both the horizontal axes.

Prolate — A spheroid which is lengthened in the polar direction (said of a rock particle). *Cf.* **Oblate.**

Prospect — The possibility or likelihood of a place that may yield mineral deposits.

Prospecting — The study of any mineral deposit for the purpose of identifying it as a possible commercial venture.

Proterozoic — The later of the two geological eons/eonothems into which the Precambrian is divided. It starts from the end of the Archaean at 2500 Ma ago to the start of the *Cambrian (*Phanerozoic), 542 Ma ago. It is divided into *Paleoproterozoic (base at 2500 Ma), *Mesoproterozoic (base at 1600 Ma) and *Neoproterozoic (base at 1000 Ma). The divisions are based on absolute ages and are arbitrary.

Protozoa — A phylum or group of phyla characterized by the absence of tissues and organs; they comprise the single-celled microscopic animals such as amoebas, flagellates, cillates and sporozoans. Fossils are known from the *Cambrian onwards.

Provenance — The source area from which the particles composing a given sediment are derived.

Psammites — *Syn.* of **Arenites**.

Psephites — *Syn.* of **Rudites.**

Pseudomorph — (1) A later mineral that has assumed the outward shape of another earlier mineral. (2) A fossil in which the original skeletal substance of the organism has been replaced by a secondary mineral in the course of fossilization, which preserves it shape.

Pteridophyta / Pteridophytes — Fern-like vascular plants that reproduce by *spores. They appeared in the *Devonian but declined during the *Mesozoic

Pterosauria — An order of the amphibians, these reptiles were highly adapted to flight; and were characterized by extreme elongation of the fourth digit of the hands for support to the wings and reduction of the hind limbs. They ranged from the Upper *Triassic to the Upper *Cretaceous.

Ptygmatic folds — Such folds have rounded *hinges and fold amplitudes nearly equal to fold wavelength; they develop in isolated layers, and are usually found in metamorphic rocks.

Pumice — A light and porous form of solidified *lava, caused by sudden release of steam or gases as it was solidifying, the material swelling up into a froth.

Pumiceous — Texture of a pyroclastic rock which is highly vesicular and presents a spongy, frothy appearance; vesicles are generally tubular.

Pyramid — A crystal form each face of which intersects the vertical axis and either two lateral axes or in the tetragonal system one lateral axis.

Pyrite — An iron disulfide, FeS_2; cubic; massive, granular; hardness 5.5 – 6.5; sp. gr. 5; brass yellow metallic luster. Also known as 'Fool's gold'.

Pyroclastic rocks — Rocks formed by the accumulation of fragmental materials or ash thrown out by volcanic explosion in the form of flows.

Pyrolusite — A grey, usually massive manganese ore of composition MnO_2; tetragonal; hardness 2–2.5; sp. gr. 4.8.

Pyroxenes — A large group of rock-forming silicate minerals, similar to *amphiboles but with a single-chain structure of silicate tetrahedral and without hydroxyl ions. Important minerals of this group are *hypersthene, *enstatite, *diopside, *augite, *pigeonite, and *jadeite.

Pyroxenite — An *ultrabasic *plutonic igneous rock composed essentially of *pyroxene with minor amounts of *hornblende, *biotite or *olivine.

Q

Quaquaversal — Said of a strata and structure that dip outward in all directions away from a central point.

Quarry — A typically large pit, open on the surface, from which stone or other minerals may be extracted. *Cf.* **Mine.**

Quartz — One of the most common minerals in the Earth's *crust. Its composition is silica (silicon dioxide, SiO_2); trigonal (hexagonal prism); hardness 7; sp. gr. 2.65. Transparent coloured varieties are considered semi-precious.

Quartzarenite — *See* **Quartzite**.

Quartzite — (1) A *granoblastic, thermally or regionally metamorphosed rock consisting mainly of quartz and formed by recrystallisation of sandstone by either thermal or regional *metamorphism. It should properly be called a **Metaquartzite**. (2) A very hard but unmetamorphosed sandstone, consisting mainly of quartz grains solidly cemented by silica that have been so completely and solidly cemented with *authigenic secondary silica that the rock breaks across or through the grain rather than around them. It was earlier described as **Orthoquartzite**, a term now in disfavour; a **Quartz arenite.**

Quaternary — According to ICS-2000 the youngest system/period of the *Cenozoic, extending from 1.75 Ma to the present, and divided into the *Pleistocene and the *Holocene series/epochs. However, in ICS-2004 the term Quaternary does not find a place, and its two divisions, *Pleistocene and *Holocene are elevated to the status of series/epochs of the redefined *Neogene. The Quaternary was characterized by extensive glaciations in the Northern Hemisphere and the emergence of mankind.

R

Radioactive dating — *Syn.* of **Radiometric dating.**

Radioactivity — The emission of ionization radiation or particles caused by the spontaneous disintegration of atomic nuclei.

Radiocarbon dating — The determination of the age of archaeological or palaeontological material by means of determining the relative proportions of isotopes of carbon-12 and carbon-14 that it contains. This method is especially useful for dating relatively recent materials, up to about 70,000 years.

Radiolaria — An informal grouping of marine single-celled *protozoa, having a typically spherical body, with an elaborate siliceous skeleton consisting of radiating spikes of silica. Their skeletons of silica have been important in forming *flint and *oozes of the ocean bottom. The range from the *Cambrian, possibly the *Precambrian, to the present.

Radiometric age — *See* **Absolute age.**

Radiometric dating — A method of dating of rocks in years by determination of the relative proportion present of 'parent' and 'daughter' *isotopes of radioactive elements. The basic principle underlying all methods is that 'parent' element decays into a stable 'daughter' element at a constant rate. The popular dating methods are : **Rubidium-strontium; Potassium-argon; Uranium-lead; Carbon-carbon (Radiocarbon).**

Raft — A fragment of rock caught up in a *magma and drifting freely, more or less vertically.

Rake — *See* **Fold.**

Range Zone — The body of strata representing the known stratigraphic and geographic range of occurrence of a particular *taxon or a combination of two taxa of any rank.

Rapakivi texture — A texture of granites in which occur relatively large oval *orthoclase crystals mantled with a soda-rich *plagioclase.

Rare earths — A group of chemically similar oxides of metals or a mixture of such oxides of elements comprising the lanthanide series (of fifteen metallic elements from lanthanum [atomic number 57] to lutetium [atomic number 71] in the Periodic Table) and usually scandium and yttrium. Rare earths are constituent of certain minerals, such as **monazite*.

Reaction rim — A zone of secondary mineral formed around a crystal.

Realgar — A soft, massive, reddish arsenic mineral, composition AsS; monoclinic; hardness 2; sp. gr. 3.6

Recent — *Syn.* of **Holocene.**

Red bole — *See* **Bole.**

Reef — (1) A ridge or chain of jagged rock, *coral, or sand just above or below the sea surface. (2) A *vein of gold or other ore. (3) A large *dyke-like body of quartz.

Refraction — The deflection of a ray of light from a straight path to its passage from one medium to another of different density as in crystals.

Refractive index — The ratio of the velocity of light in a vacuum to its velocity in a specified medium.

Refractory — A heat-resistant, hard to melt or fuse material.

Regression, Marine — The retreat of the sea from land areas, and the consequent evidence of such withdrawal, as by enlargement of the deltaic area by sedimentation. *Cf.* **Transgression, Marine.**

Reh — *See* **Kallar.**

Regolith — A layer of unconsolidated solid material covering the *bedrock.

Regur — Soil developed on top of *basaltic rocks; it is calcareous, high in montmorillonitic *clay and low in silica. Also called **Black cotton soil.**

Relative density — *Syn.* of **Specific gravity.**

Remote sensing — The procedure for collecting, processing and interpreting images recorded by aerial photographs or by imageries from artificial satellites.

Reniform — Having a kidney-shaped form or surface.

Reptilia/Reptiles — A class of air-breathing vertebrate animals that are characterize by a body covered with scales or bony plates and have ossified skeleton. They include the alligators and crocodiles, lizards, snakes, turtles and extinct related forms *dinosaurs and *pterosaurs. They first appeared in the Upper *Carboniferous and have continued up to the present.

Reserves — The amount or a supply of economic minerals or oil and natural gas that may be available for *exploitation.

Reservoir — (1) A rock strata where a fluid collects, such as water or oil and natural gas. (2) A large natural or artificial lake used as a source of water supply or for generation of electricity or for feeding irrigation canals.

Residual deposits — Soil or other deposits formed *in situ* by weathering.

Resources — A natural stock or supply of economic minerals available for possible *exploration or *exploitation.

Retrograde metamorphism — *See* **Diaphthoresis.**

Rhodochrosite — Carbonate of manganese mineral, composition $MnCO_3$; trigonal; usually massive habit; hardness 4, sp. gr. 3.7.

Rhombohedral system — A division of the *trigonal crystal system in which the unit cell is a *rhombohedron.

Rhombohedron — A solid crystal whose faces are six equal rhombuses (parallelograms with four equal sides and sometimes one with no right angles).

Rhyacian — A *geochronometric sub-division of the four-fold *Palaeoproterozoic, dated between 2300 and 2050 Ma ago, occurring after the *Siderian and before the *Orosirian.

Rhyolite — A fine-grained to glassy acid volcanic extrusive rock showing flow structures and often porphyritic.

Rhythmite — A finely laminate sediment, common in glacial lakes, in which two or three different lithologies are regularly repeated. *Cf.* **Cyclothem, Till, Tillite.**

Richter Scale — An open-ended logarithmic scale for expressing the *magnitude of an earthquake in terms of the energy dissipated in it with 1.5 indicating the weakest earthquake that can hardly be felt, while an earthquake measuring over 5 may be destructive and 8 or more is a major earthquake.

Rift valley — An enormous structural feature that forms a long trough in the Earth's *crust bounded by normal *faults. Also termed **Graben.**

Riphean — A geochronomeric sub-division of the *Precambrian, covering the time span from 1,650 to 800 Ma ago (GTS).

Ripple marks — A system or series of small parallel wavy ridges and furrows left on rock, sand or mud by the action of water or wind. The direction of current or wind is from the gently-sloping side of the ridge. The distance measured from the crest of a ripple unit to the troughs is called **ripple index.**

Road metal — Broken or crushed hard stone used in building a road. *Cf.* **Ballast.**

Roches moutonnées — A small bare outcrop rock shaped by glacial erosion with one side smooth and gently sloping and the other steep, rough and irregular.

Rock — An aggregate of one or more hard mineral material or stone of the Earth's *crust exposed on the surface or underlying the soil cover.

Rock flour — Very fine powder that is formed by abrasion of stones embedded in a glacier or ice sheet and the underlying rocks.

Rock phosphate — *See* **Phosphorite.**

Rock salt — *See* **Halite.**

Rossi-Forel (R-F) Scale — *See* **Intensity of Earthquake.**

Roundness — The degree of abrasion undergone by a *clastic particle as shown by reduction of the sharpness of its edges and corners. Along with the *spherecity it is used in **Zingg's classification** to indicate particle shape.

Royalty — The percentage of the revenue from mining or quarrying of minerals or hydrocarbons paid to the government or to the owner of the mineral rights.

Rubidium-Strontium (Rb-Sr) dating — A method of determination of absolute age in years of a mineral or rock based on the ratio of radiogenic strontium-87 to rubidium-87 and the known radioactive decay rate of rubidium-87.

Ruby — A transparent red gem variety of *corundum; refractive index 1.76/1.77–1.77/1.78; birefringence 0.008; dispersion 0.018.

Rudites — Sedimentary rocks that are gravelly and include *conglomerates, *breccias, and *tillites. *Syn.* **Psephites.**

Rutile — A black or reddish brown mineral of composition TiO_2; tetragonal; prismatic needle-like crystals; hardness 6.5; sp. gr. 4.2, 5.2.

S

Saccharoidal — A fine-grained texture of closely interlocking crystals, resembling that of granular sugar.

Salic — Denoting the silicon- and aluminium minerals of the CIPW normative classification.

Salt — A general term for naturally occurring sodium chloride (NaCl), found as *rock salt or obtained by evaporation of brine or sea water. Same as **Halite.**

Salt dome — A dome-shaped structure in sedimentary rocks, formed where a large mass of salt has been forced upwards.

Saltation — The transport of hard particles over an uneven surface in a turbulent flow of air or water by some sort of rolling and jumping action.

Sample — A fraction of a body of rock, mineral or ore obtained by approved methods for laboratory testing, analysis, or other study for determination of the nature, composition, percentage, etc., of the specified constituent, isotope, etc.

Sand — (1) A loose granular material that results from the disintegration of rocks. (2) As a size term, it is a particle between *silt and *granule, 1/16 to 2 mm in diameter.

Sand Dune — A mound or ridge of sand formed especially in a desert or along the sea coast by the action of wind.

Sandstones — Sedimentary rocks composed of grains of sand (usually *quartz) cemented together by a *matrix of usually *silica (or calcium carbonate).

Sapphire — A transparent, blue-coloured gem variety of *corundum; refractive index 1.76/1.77–1.77/1.78; birefringence 0.008; dispersion 0.018.

Saprolite — A disintegrated, weathered rock that remains in its original place retaining such original structures as jointing, banding and veining.

Sapropelic coal — *Coal that is obtained from organisms that obtain food by absorbing dissolved organic material like *spores, *algae, etc., in *anaerobic conditions.

Sard — A yellowish or brownish variety of *chalcedony.

Saturated rocks — Said of igneous rocks with neither an excess or deficiency of free *silica.

Saussurite — A compact, and white, greenish or greyish mineral aggregate consisting of a mixture of *albite (or *oligoclase) and *zoisite or *epidote, together with variable amounts of *calcite, prehnite and calcium-aluminium silicates other than those of the *epidote group; it is produced by alteration of calcic plagioclase.

Saussuritization — The process by which saussurite is formed.

Scapolites — A group of tetragonal minerals that are essentially complex silicates of aluminium, calcium and sodium; some are used as semiprecious stones.

Scaphopoda / Scaphopods — A small class of marine univalve *Mollusca with tubular shell open at both ends. They range from the Middle *Ordovician to the present; locally abundant in the *Mesozoic and the *Tertiary.

Scarp — An inclined cliff or steep, relatively straight linear face of a *cuesta or *plateau, possibly produced by faulting or *erosion.

Scheelite — A fluorescent, white, massive tungsten ore mineral, composition $CaWO_4$; tetragonal; hardness 5; sp. gr. 6.

Schiller — A bronzy iridescent play of colours shown by some minerals, particularly feldspars and pyroxenes.

Schist — A strongly folded, crystalline, low-grade regionally metamorphosed rock that can easily be split into thin flakes or slabs due to well-developed parallel or planar occurrence of majority of the constituent minerals, most of which are identifiable with the naked eye.

Schistosity — Foliation in a schist caused by platy or elongated grains, usually *micas, arranged in a parallel to sub-parallel manner, along which the rock tends to cleave.

Scoria (Pl. Scoriae) — Basaltic lava ejected as fragments from a volcano, typically with a frothy texture.

Scoriaceous — Texture of a *pyroclastic rock which is coarse and highly vesicular; *vesicles are generally spherical.

Scree — *See* **Talus**.

Scyphozoa — A class of marine *Coelenterata that comprises jellyfish lacking a true polyp and usually a velum. It ranges from the *Precambrian or *Cambrian to the present.

Sea-floor spreading — According to the theory of *plate tectonics the movement of oceanic crustal plates away from a central *mid-oceanic ridge, where new *crust is being formed by basaltic igneous rocks intruded into the fissure as the plates move apart.

Seam — (1) A thin bed, layer or stratum of valuable mineral between two distinctive layers of another kind. (2) A bed of valuable mineral, especially *coal, irrespective of thickness or position.

Secondary enrichment — *See* **Supergene enrichment.**

Secondary mineral — A mineral that occurs in a rock as a result of chemical alteration or breakdown of the original mineral as a result of weathering, solution or *metamorphism.

Sediment — Solid fragmental material that originates from weathering of rocks carried or deposited by water, wind or glacier, or accumulates by chemical action and deposited on land surface or sea bed.

Sedimentary facies — All lithological and paleontological features of a particular sedimentary rock. *See* **Facies.**

Sedimentary rock — A rock formed from the consolidation of loose *sediment and deposited in layers.

Sedimentary structure — A structure in a sedimentary rock formed either at the time of deposition or by a process subsequent to deposition. It may be on the surface, within or underside (sole) of a sedimentary unit.

Sedimentation — The action or process of forming or depositing sediment.

Sedimentology — A branch of geology concerned with the study of sediments and sedimentary rocks in all their aspects.

Seif — A sand dune in the form of a very long, narrow, sharp-crested ridge.

Seismic focus — The place deep below the Earth's surface where an *earthquake originates, and from where the vibrations spread in all directions

Seismogram — A record of Earth tremors produced by a *seismograph.

Seismograph — An instrument that measures and records details of earthquakes such as force and duration.

Seismology — The science concerned with natural earthquakes and artificially produced vibrations or tremors of the Earth.

Seismotectonics — The branch of geophysics that studies the role of seismic activity in tectonics and various other geological processes, including examination of the process leading to and accompanying *earthquakes.

Semi-precious stone — A mineral that can be used as a *gem but is considered to be less valuable than a *Precious stone.

Sequence — A succession of rocks arranged in chronologic order showing their relative position and age with respect to the geologic history as a whole.

Sequence stratigraphy — The study of rock relationships within a *chronostratigraphic framework of repetitive, genetically related *strata bounded by surfaces of *erosion or non-deposition, or their correlative conformities.

Sericite — Secondary *muscovite occurring as fine-grained flaky aggregate formed from alteration of *feldspars.

Series — A chronostratigraphic unit (rock) ranking above a **Stage** and always a division of a **System**, and found on a global scale. Its *geochronologic (time) equivalent is an **Epoch**.

Serpentine — An green, essentially hydrous magnesium silicate, $Mg_6Si_4O_{10}(OH)_8$; monoclinic; massive; hardness 2.5–4; sp. gr. 2.50 – 2.65.

Serpentinisation — The process of hydrothermal *alteration by which *ultrabasic rocks rich especially in *olivine and orthorhombic *pyroxenes are converted into or replaced by *serpentine

Shaft — A long, narrow, typically vertical hole of uniform and limited cross-section giving access to a mine for accommodating a lift, ventilation underground, raising water, etc.

Shale — A soft, fissile, finely laminated argillaceous sedimentary rock formed from consolidation of mud or clay that splits easily along bedding planes.

Shear — The strain or force produced by pressure that tends to deform a rock mass through the movement of one part of it relative to another.

Shell — The hard protective outer case of a *mollusc or *crustacean.

Shield — A very large rigid area of *Precambrian rocks unaffected by later crustal processes.

Shoe-string sand — A thin and elongated body of sediment that occurs horizontally.

Sial — The silica- and alumina-rich upper part of the Earth's *crust, composed of granitic rock types, which makes up the bulk of the continents and overlies the **Sima**.

Siderian — The oldest *geochronometric sub-division of the four-fold *Palaeoproterozoic, dated between 2500 and 2300 Ma ago, lying above the *Archaean and below the *Rhyacian.

Siderite — (1) Carbonate of iron $FeCO_3$; trigonal; hardness 4, sp. gr. 3.8–4. white, yellow and brown in colour. (2) An iron meteorite composed of almost wholly of iron alloyed with nickel.

Sief — A very large longitudinal sand dune, fairly tall, found commonly in a group,

Silica — Silicon dioxide (SiO_2), the main constituent of the Earth's *crust, occurring in nature as pure minerals or combined with other elements in silicate minerals.

Silicates — The most important group of minerals that form about 90% of the Earth's *crust. Feldspars (60%) and quartz (12%) are the most abundant. Other important silicates are *pyroxenes, *amphiboles, *micas and *olivines. The basic structural unit common to all silicate is the SiO_4 tetrahedra.

Sill — A tabular body of igneous rock intruded between and parallel with the existing strata or volcanic beds or along foliation planes of metamorphic rocks.

Sillimanite — An aluminosilicate mineral typically occurring as fibrous masses; Al_2SiO_5; orthorhombic; hardness 7; sp. gr. 3.24. It is trimorphous with **Andalusite** and **Kyanite.**

Silt — (1) A loose sedimentary material with rock particles. (2) Sediment having particle size between *clay and *sand, 1/256 – 1/16 mm in diameter.

Siltstone — A fine-grained sedimentary rock consisting of indurated *silt.

Silurian — The third higher system/period of the *Palaeozoic, between the *Ordovician and the *Devonian, lasting from about 443.7 to about 416.0 Ma ago. It is divided into four series/epoch, namely, *Llandovery, *Wenlock, *Ludlow, and *Pridoli. During this time marine fauna was generally similar to the Ordovician, although *graptolites became extinct and true jawed fish evolved; the earliest leafless land plants appeared.

Sima — The silica and magnesia rich lower part of the Earth's crust, mainly composed of basaltic rock types, which underlies the **Sial** of the continents and forms the bulk of the oceanic crust.

Sinian — According to GTS the topmost geochronometric era of the *Precambrian, lying below the *Cambrian and above the *Riphean, ranging from 800 to 570 Ma. It is divided into the lower *Sturtian and the upper *Vendian.

Sinter — A mineral deposit from a hot spring or *geyser, either calcareous (*travertine) or siliceous (*geyserite).

Skarn — Lime-bearing siliceous rock produced by the metamorphic alteration of limestone or dolomite.

Slag — A stony waste matter separated from metals during smelting or refining of ore.

Slate — A very fine-grained metamorphosed argillaceous rock having well-developed cleavage but little crystallization, resulting from low-grade regional metamorphism.

Slikensides — Small, parallel striations or grooves formed on the surface of a fault or joint plane as a result of the movement of rocks against one another. The surface of the slikenside is smooth in the movement direction, but rough in the opposite direction.

Smelting — Process of extraction of metal from its ore that involves heating and melting.

Smithsonite — A carbonate ore of zinc, composition $ZnCO_3$; trigonal; hardness 4; sp. gr. 4.4.

Soapstone — *Syn.* of **Steatite.**

Soda-lime feldspar — *Syn.* of **Plagioclase**; *Syn.* **Sodium-calcium feldspar.**

Sodalite — A transparent to translucent feldspathoid, $Na_8(AlSiO_4)_6Cl_2$; cubic; massive; hardness 6; sp. gr. 2.3.

Soil — The unconsolidated superficial layer of the Earth typically consisting of organic remains, clay, and rock particles.

Sole marks — Sedimentary structures found on the underside of a bed preserved as swellings or raised features.

Solfatara — A volcanic crater or vent containing *fumeroles that yields only hot vapour and sulfurous gases.

Solifluction — The slow and gradual creeping movement of wet soil down a slope.

Solution — The process of chemical *weathering by which rocks and minerals pass into solution by such agencies as rainwater carrying carbonic acid derived from the carbon dioxide absorbed during the passage of rain through the atmosphere.

Sorting — The process by which minerals forming a particular sediment are graded according to size by natural processes.

Sparite — Crystalline, coarse-grained calcite, or aragonite, filling the interstitial spaces in calcareous rocks.

Species — (1) A category of biological classification that is the smallest class of individuals having common attributes and designated by a common name, specifically a logical division of a *genus (*binomial classification). The name of a species (in lower case even if named after a person or locality), along with the name of the *genus it belongs to, is printed in italics. (2) A group of *minerals formally recognized as distinct from other groups.

Specific gravity — The ratio of the density of a substance to the density of pure water taken as standard when both densities are obtained by weighing in air. *Syn.* **Relative density.**

Specimen — A piece of rock, mineral, ore or fossil that is obtained from an *outcrop or sub-surface for study or display.

Speleology — The study and exploration of caves, including their deposits.

Sphalerite — A widely distributed dark coloured ore of zinc, composition ZnS; cubic; hardness 4; sp. gr. 4.1.

Sphene — A greenish, yellow or brown titanium ore mineral, $CaTiSiO_5$; monoclinic; massive; hardness 5.5; sp. gr. 3.5. A common *accessory mineral. *Syn.* **Titanite.**

Sphericity — It is a measure of the shape of a particle of sedimentary rocks, that is, the relation between its length, width and thickness. *See* **Zingg's classification** which `takes into account both *sphericity and *roundness.

Spheroclast — A rounded *phenoclast, like a cobble or pebble, in a conglomerate.

Spheroid — A spherical, or equant shape of a sedimentary particle, defined in *Zingg's classification as having width/length and thickness/width ratios greater than 2/3.

Spherule — A rounded or spherical mass of acicular crystals, commonly of *feldspars, radiating from a central point.

Spherulite — (1) A roughly spherical body or coarsely crystalline aggregate having radial structure arranged around one or more centers, of sizes ranging from microscopic grains or objects several centimeters in diameter formed *in situ* in a sedimentary rock. (2) A small (0.25–5 mm diameter) rounded particle made up of a thin calcareous layer covering a sparry calcitic core.

Spilites — Altered basaltic lavas, amygdaloidal or vesicular, containing albitic *plagiolase and in which the primary *mafic minerals have been altered to *chlorite and **Spinels.**

Spinel — A magnesium-aluminium oxide, composition $MgAl_2O_4$; cubic; hardness 8; sp. Gr. 3.6; several colours. Red spinel is a gemstone known as 'balas ruby'.

Spinel group — A continuous series of cubic oxide minerals with the general composition M3O4; they are essentially oxides of magnesium, ferrous iron, chromium, zinc, or manganese. Its important members are *magnetite (ore of iron) and *chromite (chief ore of chromium). Spinels commonly occur in ultrabasic and metamorphic rocks.

Sponges — *See* **Porifera.**

Spore — A minute, typically single-celled reproductive unit, characteristic of lower plants, *fungi and *protozoans, capable of giving rise to a new individual without sexual fusion.

Spring — A place where water gushes up or issues forth from an underground source.

Stage — Stage is the basic and normally the lowest ranking unit in the *chronostratigraphic (rock) hierarchy that can be recognized on a global scale; it is a sub-division of a **Series** and the working unit of chronostratigraphy and includes all rocks formed during its *geochronologic (time) equivalent **Age**.

Stalactite — A tapering pendant-like structure hanging from the roof of a cavern, formed of calcium salts deposited by dripping water.

Stalagmite — A mound rising from the floor of a cavern, formed of calcium salts deposited by dripping water.

Standard Global Chronostratigraphic (Geochronologic) Scale — The hierarchy of *chronostratigraphic (and their equivalent *geochronologic units) of world-wide scope which provides a standard scale of reference for the dating of rocks everywhere and for relating all rocks everywhere to world geologic history.

Statherian — The youngest geochronometric sub-division of the four-fold *Palaeoproterozoic, dated between 1800 and 1600 Ma ago, lying above the *Orosirian and below the *Calymmian.

Staurolite — A brown iron-aluminium silicate, $FeAl_4Si_2O_{10}(OH)_2$; orthorhombic; prismatic crystals; hardness 7; sp. gr. 3.7.

Steatite — The mineral *talc occurring in massive form. Also called **Soapstone.**

Steel — An alloy of iron with essential carbon and usually other elements which categorize its variety.

Stellate — Made up of fibers and columns radiating from a center, producing star-like forms.

Stenian — The upper *geochronometric sub-division of the *Mesoproterozoic, dated between 1200 and 1000 Ma ago, lying above the *Ectasian and below the *Tonian.

Stibnite. A metallic silver grey sulphide of antimony, composition Sb_2S_3; orthorhombic, prismatic: hardness 2; sp. gr. 4.6.

Stone — (1) A hard, solid nonmetallic mineral matter of which a rock is made. (2) In the gem trade, a cut and polished mineral used for jewellery.

Stony meteorite — A general term for meteorites consisting mostly or entirely of silicate minerals, chiefly *olivine, *pyroxene and *plagioclase (chondrite, achrondite) *Syn.* **Aerolite.**

Stope — A usually step-like excavation underground for the removal of *ore that is formed as the ore is mined in successive layers.

Stratification — The form shown by sedimentary rocks in being disposed in parallel layers or *beds, called *strata.

Stratigraphic classification — The systematic zonation of the rock strata of the Earth's crust in normal sequence into units with reference to any or all of the characters, properties or attributes which rocks may possess which may be on the basis of *lithology, *paleontology, magnetic property or any other criteria.

Stratigraphic unit — A *stratum or an assemblage of strata recognized as a unit in the classification of the Earth's rock sequence with respect to any rock character, property or attribute.

Stratigraphy — The branch of geology concerned with the order, succession and relative dating of *strata.

Stratotype — The designated exposure of named layered *stratigraphic unit or of a stratigraphic boundary that serves as a standard reference. Also called **Type Section.**

Stratum (Pl. **Strata**) — A layer of rock characterized by certain unifying characters, properties or attributes distinguishing it from adjacent layers. Also *See* **Bed**.

Streak — The colour of the fine powder of a mineral having nonmetallic luster obtained by scratching or rubbing against a piece of unglazed porcelain.

Striations — Lines that have been etched or scratched into rock surface over which a *glacier has passed.

Strike — (1) The horizontal or the compass direction of a stratum, fault or other geological feature perpendicular to the direction of the **Dip**. (2) Loosely used for the general trend of a bed or tabular body.

Stromatolite — An organo-sedimentary structure formed mainly by the blue-green algae that occurs generally in calcareous, phosphatic or cherty sedimentary rocks. It is now widely regarded as a fossil and is given Linnean binomial names.

Stromatoporoid — A general term for a group of extinct benthenic marine organisms of uncertain biological affinities.

Strontianite — Carbonate mineral, $SrCO_3$; orthorhombic; prismatic habit; fibrous to massive; hardness 3.5–4; sp. gr. 3.7; colour grey, yellowish, greenish.

Structural geology — The branch of geology that is concerned with the form, arrangement and structural features of the rocks on moderate to small scale. *Cf.* **Tectonics.**

Structure — (1) The overall structural features of an area, such as *unconformities, *folds and *faults. (2) A megascopic feature of a rock body in the outcrop. (3) The form assumed by a mineral, such as tabular or fibrous.

Stuartian — The lower of the two geochronometric periods of the *Sinian, lasting from 800 to 610 Ma (GTS).

Stylolite — A surface or contact, usually occurring in homogeneous carbonate rocks (rarely in sandstones and quartzites) that is marked by an irregular and teeth-like interlocking penetration of the two sides; a stylolite is usually parallel or subparallel to the bedding plane, but rarely it may be cross-cutting; it is sometimes mineralized along the suture.

Subanthracite coal — A coal in rank between *bituminous coal and *anthracite.

Subautomorphic — *Syn.* of **Subhedral**.

Sub-bituminous coal — A coal intermediate in rank between *lignite and *bituminous coal, distinguished from lignite by higher carbon and lower moisture content.

Subduction zone — According to the theory of *plate tectonics it is a region in which one crustal plate of the Earth is forced down, i.e., subducted, beneath another and moves down into the mantle where it is eventually assimilated.

Subgroup — A sub-division of a group which may consist of related formations not large enough to form a *group; a formally differentiated assemblage of formations within a group.

Subhedral — Said of a crystal that has poorly developed crystal faces or partly bounded by crystal faces. *Syn.* **Subidiomorphic; Subautomorphic; Hypidiomorphic; Hypautomorphic.**

Subidiomorphic — Same as **Subhedral**.

Submarine canyon — A steep-sided, V-type valley often heading in the continental shelf running down the continental slope in the sea resembling a river-cut land canyon.

Subperiod — A *geochronologic unit that is a portion of the *Period, but longer than an *Epoch during which the rocks of the *Subsystem were formed.

Substage — A sub-division of a *Stage; the lowest unit of the conventional hierarchy of formal *chronostratigraphic units.

Subsurface — The zone below the surface of the Earth, whose geologic features, like stratigraphic and structural, are interpreted on the basis of drill records and various types of geophysical evidence.

Subsystem — A formally established sub-division of a *System (such as the *Mississippian Subsystem of the *Carboniferous System)

Succession — A number of rock units or mass of *strata that succeed one another in chronologic order in a stratigraphic section or area.

Supercontinent — A former large land mass believed to have split and drifted away in the geological past to form some of the present continents. *See* **Gondwanaland;** and **Laurasia.**

Superficial deposits — Extraneous material transported and deposited by various geomorphological processes that lies on top of solid older rocks.

Supergene — Said of enrichment of a mineral deposit formed near the surface, commonly by descending solutions that leach metals, carry them downward, and precipitate them, thus enriching sulphide minerals already present. *Syn.* **Secondary enrichment.**

Supergroup — A *lithostratigraphic unit comprising two or more associated *groups and /or *formations.

Superposition — The principle that if one set of strata occur on top of another in a succession the upper unit was formed later, except in the case of overturned strata by tectonic action.

Supersequence — One or more sequences that are bounded by unconformities of the first order, i.e., related to major tectonic events of global nature, such as magnetism, eustatic and climatic changes and metamorphism.

Supracrustal — Refers to rocks that **ovelie** the *basement rocks or at the surface of the Earth. *Cf.* **Infracrustal.**

Suture — A *fault that marks the boundary between two crustal blocks that were once widely separated, often on different *plates. It indicates that oceanic *lithosphere once existed between two blocks.

Syenite — A coarse-grained *plutonic igneous rock composed essentially of alkali *feldspars with accessory *quartz up to 5% and *ferromagnesian minerals which are used to qualify and naming various kinds of syenites.

Syenitoid — A preliminary field term suggested for a *plutonic igneous rock with less than 20% *quartz or less than 10% *feldspar.

Syenodiorite — *Syn.* of **Monzonite.**

Syncline — **A** concave flexture of stratified rocks forming a trough with its limbs dipping inwards and in which the younger beds form the core with the strata getting older outwards towards the base or bottom. It is opposite of **Anticline.**

Syneclise — A negative or depressed suture of a broad and enormous continental platform produced by slow crustal downwarp during the course of several geologic periods.

Synform — A concave flexture of stratified rocks forming a trough with its limbs dipping inwards, but the stratigraphic sequence of its beds is not known. Opposite of **Antiform.**

Syntaxis — A sharp bend in an *orogenic belt or mountain chain accompanied by fraying into several strands.

Syntype — Each of a set of type specimens of a fossil upon which the description and name of a new species is jointly based.

System — It is a chronostratigraphic (rock) unit of major rank on a global scale, above a *Series and below an *Erathem. Its geochronologic (time) equivalent is a **Period**.

T

Tabular — (1) Said of a relatively broad and thin crystal with two well-developed parallel faces. (2) A feature that is broad and flat like the top of a table.

Taconite — A bedded and banded ferruginous cherty rock. *Cf.* **Banded iron formation.**

Talc — A very soft basic silicate of magnesium, $Mg_3Si_4O_{10}(OH)_2$; monoclinic; massive; hardness 1; sp. gr. 2.7; soapy feel. *Syn.* **Steatite**; it forms the rock **Soapstone.**

Talus — An accumulation of various sizes and shapes of rock fragments derived from mechanical destruction of outcropping rock on its steep slope. *Syn.* **Scree.**

Taphonomy — The branch of paleontology concerned with the process of fossilization, such as burial, decay, and preservation of organic bodies.

Taphrogeny/Taphrogenesis — A general term for the formation of rift phenomena, characterized by high-angle normal faulting and associated subsidence.

Taphrogeosyncline — *Syn.* of **Rift valley.**

Taxon (Pl. **Taxa**) — A group of organisms of whatever rank, such as a particular species, genus, family or class.

Taxonomy — The branch of science concerned with classification of animals and plants according to their presumed natural relationships.

Tectogene — A down-buckling of the Earth's crust that results in the down-buckling of granitic rocks deep into the Earth's crust to form roots of mountains; also results in formation of orogenic mountain belts.

Tectonics — A branch of geology concerned with the study of the structure of the Earth's crust, particularly such processes as movement of rock bodies during folding and faulting.

Tectonophysics — The branch of geophysics that deals with the forces which cause movement and deformation in the Earth's *crust.

Tektite — A small black glassy object found over certain areas of the Earth's surface believed to have been formed as molten debris in *meteorite impact and scattered widely through the air.

Tellurite — A mineral of tellurium, composition TeO_2; orthorhombic; hardness 2; sp. gr. 5.9.

Tenor — The general quantity or percentage of economic metal or mineral content of an *ore or mineral deposit.

Tephra — Fragmental material thrown out by volcanic explosion, expelled as solid fragments or in molten state.

Terrace — A natural horizontal embankment or shelf-like formation such as a raised beach.

Terrain (Terrane) — A stretch of land surface over which a particular rock or group of rocks is prevalent.

Tertiary — An older name for the *Cenozoic, though the two are not coterminous, referring as they do to different time spans. The term survives from long and is entrenched in older geological literature. For long, it was considered as older of the two divisions of the Cenozoic, the younger being the *Quaternary. Incidentally, both terms have now been abandoned in the new ICS-2004. Classical Tertiary comprised the *Palaeocene, *Eocene, *Oligocene, *Miocene, and *Pliocene.

Tethys — An geosynclinal ocean that developed between *Laurasia and *Gondwanaland during the *Mesozoic. It disappeared as a result of *seafloor spreading when the Alpine-Himalayan mountain chains were formed.

Tetragonal system — A crystal system in which the three axes are mutually at right angles, two horizontal ones being equal and the vertical either smaller or greater than the other two. It has seven symmetry classes.

Texture — The small-scale structure recognized in rocks, originating from the geometrical relationship of minerals constituting the rock. It depends on four factors : (i) grain size, (ii) grain shape,

(iii) degree of crystallinity, and (iv) contact relationship of the grains.

Thanatocoenosis — An assemblage of fossils composed of the remains of animals that have been brought together by various agencies after their death by sedimentary processes and thus may not have lived together. Thus, most fossil occurrences may be considered thanatocoenoses.

Theory — An explanatory system of propositions or general principles inferred from phenomena and linking known facts and observations held to be true until contradicted or amended by new facts or observations. Theory is more firmly founded than a *Hypothesis.

Thin section — A thin slice of rock cut and ground to a standard thickness of 0.33 mm and mounted on a glass slide for study under a *polarising microscope.

Tholeiite — A *basalt consisting of basic *plagioclase and *pyroxene (pigeonite) with interstitial glass or quartz-alkali feldspar *intergrowth.

Throw — The amount of vertical displacement of blocks on either side of a *fault.

Thrust — A kind of reverse fault with low angle that extends over a large distance. In thrusting, a large crustal unit rides over another, with the overriding block moving upward as it passes over the lower block.

Till — A sediment or drift consisting of an unstratified and unsorted deposit of *clay, *gravel and *boulders left behind after retreat of glaciers and ice sheets. *Syn.* **Boulder clay**.

Tillite — A sedimentary rock that is lithified **Till**.

Time — The measured or measurable period during which a geological process took place.

Titanite — *Syn.* of **Sphene.**

Tongue — It is projecting part of a *stratigraphic unit extending beyond its main body.

Tonian — The lower *geochronometric sub-division of the *Neoproterozoic, dated between 1000 and 850 Ma ago, lying above the *Stenian and below the *Cryogenian.

Topaz — A silicate mineral, composition $Al_2SiO_4(OH,F)_2$; orthorhombic; prismatic; hardness 8; sp. gr. 3.5; yellow-transparent variety is used as a gem.

Topographic map — A map on a stated scale to show the detailed surface features of an area, including relief (usually by contours) and natural and man-made features.

Topography — The configuration of a land surface including its relief and position of its natural and man made features.

Topotype — Any specimen of a fossil collected from the locality from which the *type specimen was obtained.

Topset — *See* **Cross bedding.**

Tourmaline — A complex borosilicate mineral; trigonal; prismatic; hardness 7; sp. gr. 3.1; black; when transparent and cut makes a striking gem.

Trace — A similar term to **Trend**, but it signifies the intersection of a geological surface with another surface, like the trace of bedding on a *fault surface or the trace of a fault or *outcrop on the ground.

Trace element — A chemical element present only in minute amounts.

Trace fossils — Sedimentary strictures resulting from biological activities. Though not fossils in a strict sense, the product of these activities are so regarded and named according to Linnean system. These structures include burrows and other excavations, tracks, trails, footprints, evidence of feeding activities, etc. *Syn.* **Ichnofossils**.

Trachyte — A group of fine-grained extrusive igneous rocks, generally porphyritic, consisting mainly of alkali *feldspar and minor *mafic minerals.

Transgression, Marine — Flooding of large land area by marine water during a short geological time, and the consequent evidence of such advance, often by deposition of strata unconformably on older rocks. *Cf.* **Regression.**

Transportation — An aspect of *sedimentation that covers the movement of any loose material by natural agencies, such as flowing water, wind or gravity, from one place to another.

Transverse thrust — Same as **Transcurrent fault.**

Trap — (1) A dark-coloured, fine-grained basaltic extrusive rock. (2) In petroleum geology, a barrier to the upward movement of oil or gas, allowing them to accumulate.

Travertine — A white or light-coloured calcareous rock deposited from mineral springs.

Tremolite — *See* **Actinolite.**

Trench — A narrow, elongate depression of the deep-sea floor associated with a *subduction zone. It is oriented parallel to a volcanic arc and commonly to the edge of the continent, between the continental margin and the abyssal hills.

Trend — A general term for the alignment, direction or bearing of an *outcrop, *dyke, *vein, linear *ore body, *fold, etc. *Cf.* **Trace.**

Triassic — The earliest of the three systems/periods of the *Mesozoic extending from about 251.0 to about 199.6 Ma ago. It is divided into three series/epochs. During this time widespread desert conditions obtained, with the hot climate becoming warm and wet. *Pangea broke into the southern *supercontinent of *Gondwanaland and northern of *Laurasia. During this time ichthyosaurs, flying fish and *crustaceans appeared. It was characterized by the first appearance of *dinosaurs and small mammals. Plant life was mainly primitive *gymnosperms with dominant ferns and *conifers.

Triclinic system — A crystal system that has three axes, of which none are at right angles to any other and are unequal. There is no plane and no axis of symmetry, but symmetry solely with respect to the central point. It has two classes of symmetry.

Trigonal system — A crystal system considered either a division of the *hexagonal system or an independent system, according to different authorities. *Syn.* **Rhombohedral.**

Trilobita / Trilobites — A class of numerous extinct marine *arthropods having segments of the body divided by furrows on the dorsal surface into three lobes. They ranged from the Lower *Cambrian to *Permian, though they declined from the *Ordovician onwards.

True north — The direction from any point on the Earth's surface towards the geographic north pole; it is 0° or 360° on the compass direction.

Tufa — A porous rock composed of calcium carbonate and formed by precipitation from water.

Tuff — A light porous rock formed by consolidation of volcanic **Ash**.

Turbidites — Sedimentary rocks ranging from *siltstones to *sandstones and *grits characterized by *graded bedding and moderate *sorting said to be deposited by *turbidity currents.

Turbidity current — An underwater density current flowing swiftly down a subaquous slope owing to the weight of the sediment it carries, and spreading horizontally on the floor of the body of water.

Twin — A composite crystal in which two individual crystals have different orientation in simple crystallographic relationship to each other.

Twin, Penetration — A *twin in which two crystals penetrate each other.

Twin axis — The axis of symmetry about which an individual in a twined crystal can be rotated to produce the orientation of the other.

Twin plane — The plane of symmetry in which an individual in a twinned crystal can be reflected to produce the orientation of the other.

Twinning — The state of a crystal that is a composite consisting of two or more parts of the same crystal species which are reversed in orientation with respect to each other.

Twinning, Carlsbad — A twinning in feldspar, especially orthoclase, in which the twin axis is the crystallographic axis.

Twinning, Laminar — A type of twinning in which the two twin orientations are equally likely to be adopted and are often found as closely spaced lamelle. *Syn.* **Polysynthetic twinning.**

Twinning, Polysynthetic — Repeated twinning of three or more individuals on parallel composition planes. *Syn.* **Lamillar twinning; Multiple twinning.**

Type section — *Syn.* of **Stratotype**.

Type specimen — The specimen, or each of a set of specimens, on which the description and name of a new species of a fossil is based. *See* also **Holotype**; **Syntype.**

U

Ultrabasic rocks — Rocks that are free of quartz, *feldspars and *feldspathoids, and are essentially composed of *ferro-magnesian minerals. Most ultrabasic rocks are *ultramafic but some monomineralic rocks composed, say, of *pyroxenes, are not ultrabasic because of their high silica content. Ultramafic rocks that contain 90–100 per cent *mafic and related minerals and are very dark coloured.

Ultramafic rocks — *See* **Ultrabasic rocks**.

Unconformity — A surface of erosion or contact between rock bodies representing a significant break or gap in the stratigraphic sequence. There are several kinds of unconformities and they are described under various heads.

Unconformity, Angular — The unconformity is characteristic of sedimentary rocks that are laid upon previously tilted or folded strata; bedding planes below and above the unconformity surface are at an angle to each other.

Undersaturated rocks — Igneous rocks that are deficient in silica and contain *feldspathoids and *olivine, or olivine and *hypersthene.

Underthrust — A low-angled fault resulting in the movement of the *footwall relative to the *hanging wall.

Uniaxial — Said of a crystal having only one optic axis, such as that belonging to tetragonal or hexagonal crystal systems. This property is studied under the polarizing microscope.

Uniformitarianism — The principle that geological processes controlling the evolution of the Earth's crust were of the same kind throughout geological times as they are today. First proposed by British geologist James Hutton.

Unsaturated — Said of a mineral that cannot develop in the presence of free *silica.

Upheaval — An upward displacement of a part of the Earth's *crust.

Upland — An area of high or hilly land.

Uplift — An island, mountain, etc., created by an upward movement of a portion of the Earth's surface.

Upper — The qualifying term applied to the name of a *chronostratigraphic unit (*System, *Series, *Stage) to indicate position in the geologic column; it corresponds to *Late as applied to the name of the equivalent geologic time units (*Period, *Epoch, *Age).

Upper mantle — The part of the mantle which lies above the depth of about 670 km and has a density of 3.4 g/cm^3 to 4.0 g/cm^3 with increasing depth.

Upthrow — The amount of the upward vertical displacement of a *fault block.

Uraninite — Main ore of uranium, composition UO_2; cubic octahedral; hardness 5.5; sp. gr. 9–9.7.

Uranium-lead (U-Pb) dating — A method of calculating the absolute age in years for minerals and rocks based on the known radioactive decay rate of uranium-238 to lead-206 and uranium-235 to lead-207.

V

Varanger — The lower *geochronometric epoch of the *Vendian, between 610 and 590 Ma ago (GTS).

Varve — A thin layer of sediment, usually clay or silt, of contrasting colour and texture in glacial lakes that represent the deposit of a single year. Varves occur in pairs in a rhythmic manner annually.

Vascular plants — Plants with vascular tissue, having a specialized conducting system that includes xylem and phloem; included are flowering plants, conifers, cycads, ferns, horsetails and clubmosses.

Vaterite — A rare, unstable hexagonal carbonate mineral, $CaCO_3$; trimorphous with *calcite and *aragonite.

Vein — A tabular of sheet-like body of minerals which has been intruded into a *joint or *fissure, or a system of joints and fissures, in rocks.

Vendian — The upper *geochronometric period of the *Sinian covering the time span between 610 and 570 Ma. It is divided into the lower *Varanger, and the upper *Ediacara (GTS).

Vermiculite — A yellow or brown micaceous, layer-lattice, hydrous silicate of aluminium, magnesium or iron of widely varying composition; alteration product of mica; light weight, highly water absorbent and expands enormously on heating.

Vertebrata / Vertebrates — A subphylum of *Chordata possessing a spinal column that includes mammals, birds, reptiles, amphibians, and fishes.

Vesicle — A small, rounded cavity in a volcanic rock produced by gas bubbles during solidification.

Vesicular — Said of an igneous rock in which spherical, ovoid or tubular openings occur.

Vitrain — A major coal material which is brilliant, of vitreous luster, black in colour and forms the major constituent of *bituminous coal; it occurs in very thin bands or lenticles less than 5mm thick.

Volcanic bomb — A rounded pyroclast ejected from a volcano which forms when the viscous lava is in flight.

Volcanic glass — *See* **Obsidian.**

Volcanic neck — An erosional remnant of a vertical pipe-like intrusion that represents a former vent.

Volcanic pipe — A breccia-filled vertical conduit through the Earth's *crust through which magmatic materials have passed in a *volcano.

Volcanic plug — A filling of lava in a volcanic crater that has been exposed by *erosion.

Volcanic rocks — Fine-grained and/or glassy igneous rocks formed due to volcanic action extruded at or near the Earth's surface. *Syn.* **Extrusive rocks**.

Volcano — A mountain or a hill having a crater or a vent through which *lava, rock fragments, hot vapour and gas are or have been erupted through the Earth's *crust.

Volcanology (Vulcanology) — The scientific study of *volcanoes and their products.

Vug (Vugh) — A cavity in a volcanic rock lined with secondary mineral crystals.

W

Wacke — A sandstone of which the clay and fine silt matrix in which the poorly-sorted grains are embedded amounts to 15–75% of the mass.

Wall-rock — (1) The rock body comprising the wall of a *fault. (2) The rock adjacent to a mineral deposit or igneous intrusion.

Wall-rock alteration — Changes in the country rock adjacent to *hydrothermal *ore *deposits by the fluids responsible for or derived during the formation of the deposits.

Water — (1) A large part of water occurs on and within the Earth, and it is regarded as a geological material. The humble H_2O also plays an important role in geological processes, like *sedimentation and *weathering. Also *See* *Spring; *Water table. (2) Said of the degree of clarity and *lustre of a *gem stone.

Water, Artesian — Confined ground water under pressure much grater than that of the atmosphere which issues forth without pumping.

Water, Connate — Water that was imprisoned in a sedimentary rock when it was originally deposited.

Water, Juvenile — Water derived on the Earth's surface from a deep underground magmatic source, such as volcanic emanation, or associated with igneous intrusion.

Water, Meteoric — Water that originated on the surface derived from the atmosphere and percolated down.

Water, Phreatic — *Groundwater that occurs in the upper part of the saturated zone under *water table conditions (below the water table), that is, where all fissures are filled with groundwater; they supply springs and wells. Often considered a synonym of *Ground water.

Watershed — An area or region bounded peripherally by a divide of higher ground and ultimately draining to a particular water course or body of water.

Water table — The level or surface below which the ground is saturated with water.

Weathering — The process of breakdown and alteration of rocks on the Earth's surface due to chemical and mechanical actions. The main agencies of weathering are water, wind, and ice.

Welded tuff — *See* **Ignimbrite**.

Wenlock — A series / epoch of the four-fold *Silurian, lying above the *Llandovery and under the *Ludlow, and extending from about 428.2 to about 422.9 Ma. It consists of two stages.

Wilson cycle — A successive reoccurrence of *plate-tectonic spreading and convergence with a period generally in the 100-million year range.

Wind — It is a basic element of the weather and therefore of *weathering.

Window — An enclosed area of a *thrust sheet or a *recumbent fold that exposes the younger rocks beneath because of *denudation of the older rocks above. *Syn.* **Fenster**.

Witherite — A carbonate mineral of barium, composition $BaCO_3$; orthorhombic; pseudo-hexagonal twinned crystals; hardness 3.5; sp. gr. 4.3.

Wolframite — A source of tungsten, composition $(Fe,Mn)WO_4$; monoclinic; hardness 5; sp. gr. 7.3.

Wollastonite — A calcium silicate mineral; composition $CaSiO_3$; triclinic; hardness 5; sp. gr. 2.9.

X

Xenoblast — A mineral that has grown during *metamorphism without development of its characteristic crystal faces.

Xenocryst — A commonly *anhedral crystal that resembles a *phenocryst but is foreign to the body of the igneous rock in which it occurs.

Xenolith — An inclusion of a foreign unassimilated rock, irrespective of its size, that occurs in an igneous rock body. *Syn.* **Accidental inclusion**.

Xenomorphic — *See* **Allotriomorphic**.

X-ray diffraction pattern — The characteristic interference pattern obtained when X-rays are diffracted by a crystal that may be utilized for mineral identification.

Y

Yardang — Steep-sided, undercut, overhanging furrowed ridges of rock sculptured by wind-borne sands in a desert.

Younging — Said of a series of beds arranged oldest to youngest from bottom to top to indicate their order of superposition.

Z

Zeolites — A large group of hydrous silicate minerals that have structures similar to *feldspars and *feldspathoids, and occur as secondary filling in cavities of lavas.

Zeugen — The tabular mass of rock which consists of a pedestal of relatively soft rock capped by a layer of more resistant rock, resulting from differential erosion by wind-borne sand.

Zeugogeosyncline — A *parageosyncline with marginal uplifts.

Zingg's shape classification — This is a fourfold classification of pebbles in rudaceous sedimentary rocks taking into account the total function of their *sphericity and *roundness; based on graphical representation of the diameter ratio of width to length plotted against the diameter ratio of thickness to width.

Class number	*Breadth/ length*	*Thickness/ breadth*	*Shape*
I	> 2/3	< 2/3	Oblate (Discoidal)
II	> 2/3	> 2/3	Equiaxial; (Spheroidal)
III	< 2/3	< 2/3	Triaxial (Bladed)
IV	< 2/3	> 2/3	Prolate (Rod-shaped)

Zircon — A typically brown, but sometimes in transparent gem form, mineral of composition $ZrSiO_4$; tetragonal; prismatic; hardness 7.5; sp. gr. 4.3; often found as a detrital mineral.

Zoisite — Basic silicate of calcium and aluminium, $Ca_2Al_3Si_3O_{12}(OH)$; orthorhombic; hardness 6–6.5; sp. gr. 3.3; related to *epidote.

Zone — A minor interval in any category of stratigraphic classification.

Zoning — Straight growth lines of bands with definite angles often seen in crystals. If seen in transparent or translucent crystals, particularly in gemstones, it indicates that the stone is of natural origin.

ANNEXURE

ANNEXURE

International Stratigraphic Column

This column has been adapted from the International Statigraphic Chart of the International Commission on Stratigraphy 2004 and other sources. The isotopic ages show the base in million years.

Series / Epoch names are in **Bold *italic***, and Stage / Age names are in ordinary *italics.*

The date of a stage that is also the base date of the relevant system / period is underlined.

PHANEROZOIC (Eonothem/Eon)

CENOZOIC (Erathem / Era)	***Age (Ma)***
Neogene (System/Period)	
Holocene	0.0115
Pleistocene	
Upper	0.126
Middle	0.781
Lower	1.806

Pliocene	
Gelasian	2.588
Piacenzian	3.600
Zanclean	5.332
Miocene *23.03*	
Messinian	7.246
Tortonian	11.608
Serravallian	13.65
Langhian	15.97
Burdigalian	20.43
Aquitanian	23.03

Paleogene (System / Period)

Oligocene	
Chattian	28.04 ± 0.1
Rupelian	33.9 ± 0.1
Eocene	
Priabonian	37.2 ± 0.1
Bartonian	40.4 ± 0.2
Lutetian	48.6 ± 0.2
Ypresian	55.8 ± 0.2
Paleocene	
Thanetian	58.7 ± 0.2
Selandian	61.7 ± 0.2
Danian	65.5 + 0.3

MESOZOIC (Erathem / Era)

Cretaceous (System / Period)

Upper / Late Cretaceous	
Maastrichtian	70.6 ± 0.6
Campanian	83.5 ± 0.7
Santonian	85.8 ± 0.7
Coniacian	89.3 ± 1.0
Turonian	93.5 ± 0.8
Cenomanian	99.6 ± 0.9

Lower / Early Cretaceous

Stage	Age
Albian	112.0 ± 1.0
Aptian	125.0 ± 1.0
Barremian	130.0 ± 1.5
Hauterivian	136.4 ± 2.0
Valanginian	140.2 ± 3.0
Berriasian	145.5 ± 4.0

Jurassic (System / Period)

Upper / Late Jurassic

Stage	Age
Tithonian	150.8 ± 4.0
Kimmeridgian	155.7 ± 4.0
Oxfordian	161.2 ± 4.0

Middle Jurassic

Stage	Age
Callovian	164.7 ± 4.0
Bathonian	167.7 ± 3.5
Bajocian	171.6 ± 3.0
Aalenian	175.6 ± 2.0

Lower / Early Jurassic

Stage	Age
Toarcian	183.0 ± 1.5
Pilensbachian	189.6 ± 1.5
Sinemurian	196.5 ± 1.0
Hettangian	199.6 ± 0.6

Triassic (System / Period)

Upper / Late Triassic

Stage	Age
Rhaetian	203.6 ± 1.5
Norian	216.5 ± 2.0
Carnian	228.0 ± 2.0

Middle Triassic

Stage	Age
Ladinian	237.0 ± 2.0
Anisian	245.0 ± 1.5

Lower / Early Triassic

Stage	Age
Olenekian	249.7 ± 0.7
Induan	251.0 ± 0.4

PALEOZOIC (Erathem /Era)

Permian (system/period)

Lopingian	
Changhsingian	253.8 ± 0.7
Wuchiapingian	260.4 ± 0.7
Guadalupian	
Capitanian	265.8 ± 0.7
Wordian	268.0 ± 0.7
Roadian	270.6 ± 0.7
Cisuralian	
Kungurian	275.6 ± 0.7
Artinskian	284.4 ± 0.7
Sakmarian	294.6 ± 0.8
Asselian	299.0 ± 0.8

Carboniferous (System / Period)

Pennsylvanian (Subsystem / Sub period)

Upper / Late Pennsylvanian	
Gzhelian	303.9 ± 0.9
Kasimovian	306.5 ± 1.0
Middle Pennsylvanian	
Moscovian	311.7 ± 1.1
Lower / Early Pennsylvanian	
Bashkirian	318.1 ± 1.3

Mississippian (Subsystem / Sub period)

Upper / Late Mississippian	
Serpukhovian	326.4 ± 1.6
Middle Mississippian	
Visean	345.3 ± 2.1
Lower / Early Mississippian	
Tournaisian	359.2 ± 2.5

Unit	Age
Devonian (System / Period)	
Upper / Late Devonian	
Famennian	374.5 ± 2.6
Frasnian	385.3 ± 2.6
Middle Devonian	
Givetian	391.8 ± 2.7
Eifelian	397.5 ± 2.7
Lower / Early Devonian	
Emsian	407.0 ± 2.8
Pragian	411.2 ± 2.8
Lochkovian	416.0 ± 2.8
Silurian (System / Period)	
Pridoli	418.7 ± 2.7
Ludlow	
Ludfordian	421.3 ± 2.6
Gorstian	422.9 ± 2.5
Wenlock	
Homerian	426.2 ± 2.4
Sheinwoodian	428.2 ± 2.3
Llandovery	
Telychian	436.0 ± 1.9
Aeronian	439.0 ± 1.8
Rhuddanian	443.7 ± 1.5
Ordovician	
Upper / Late Ordovician	460.9 ± 1.6
Middle Ordovician	471.8 ± 1.6
Lower Ordovician	488.3 ± 1.7
Cambrian	
Furongian	501.0 ± 2.0
Middle Cambrian	513.0 ± 2.0
Lower / Early Cambrian	542.0 ± 1.0

PRECAMBRIAN	
PROTEROZOIC (Eonothem / Eon)	
NEOPROTEROZOIC (Erathem / Era)	
Edicaran (System / Period)	630
Cryogenian (System / Period)	850
Tonian (System / Period)	1000
MESOPROTEROZOIC (Erathem / Era)	
Stenian (System / Period)	1200
Ectasian (System / Period)	1400
Calymmian (System / Period)	1600
PALEOPROTEOROZOIC (Erathem / Era)	
Statherian (System / Period)	1800
Orosirian (System / Period)	2050
Rhyacian (System / Period)	2300
Siderian (System / Period)	2500
ARCHEAN (Eonothem / Eon)	
NEOARCHEAN (Erathem / Era)	2800
MESOARCHEAN (Erathem / Era)	3200
PALEOARCHEAN (Erathem / Era)	3600
EOARCHEAN (Erathem / Era)	3850?
HADEAN (Eonothem / Eon) (Lower limit not defined)	4560?